Time of Apprenticeship | *The Fiction of Young James Joyce*

James Joyce and his grandson, Stephen

Time of Apprenticeship | *The Fiction of Young James Joyce*

BY MARVIN MAGALANER

BOOKS FOR LIBRARIES PRESS
FREEPORT, NEW YORK

INTERNATIONAL STANDARD BOOK NUMBER:
0-8369-5609-5

LIBRARY OF CONGRESS CATALOG CARD NUMBER:
70-140366

PRINTED IN THE UNITED STATES OF AMERICA

To my Mother and Father

James Joyce's apprenticeship as a literary craftsman, in spite of its importance, has been too little studied. This book represents a start toward a full-length, close analysis of Joyce's craftsmanship during his younger days. In writing it, I have chosen to draw most of my illustrative examples from the short stories of *Dubliners* since this work has been so thoroughly ignored by critics. Also, in order to give the textual study a living background, I have included a sketch of the artist's life during this important period.

My gratitude to the persons and institutions that have given me aid and comfort in writing about Joyce is very strong. Professor William York Tindall of Columbia University helped in improving a primitive version of Chapters III and V; more generally, however, he is responsible for my professional interest in Joyce. Mr. Allan Angoff, former Editor of New York University Press, has given me, over the past three years, patient, unerring advice. I am also indebted to Mr. Philip L. Handler for his kindness in allowing me to read his unpublished essay on *Stephen Hero* and *A Portrait*; to Mr. Herbert Cahoon of the Morgan Library for answers to questions about Joyce; to Mr. John J. Slocum for letting me examine many unpublished manuscripts of the stories of *Dubliners*; and to Dr. Brooks Wright of the City College of New York for good advice. I am most grateful to Dr. Julian B. Kaye of Brooklyn College and to Dr. Arthur Zeiger of the City College of New York, who read this book in manuscript and offered excellent suggestions.

Those who hold the rights to publish many of the quotations in this book have been generous in giving permission. Miss Harriet Weaver and Mr. Lionel Monro, acting for the administrators of the Joyce estate, have graciously allowed quotations from early manuscript versions of Joyce's stories and from the letters of Joyce to Robert McAlmon. Mrs. William Butler Yeats generously permitted me to publish several letters from her husband to Joyce. I am grateful to Dorothy and Ezra Pound for permission to quote from a letter of Mr. Pound to James B. Pinker; and to Lord Horder, Director of Gerald Duckworth & Co., for the right to publish the 1916 report of the firm's reader on Joyce's *A Portrait*. Professor Norman Holmes Pearson of Yale University let me use the Joyce-McAlmon correspondence from his collection before publication. I am indebted to Nancy Rothwax for the photograph used as frontispiece.

My sincere thanks go to *Modern Fiction Studies*, to *Modern Language Notes* and the Johns Hopkins Press, and to *PMLA* for permission to use adaptations of articles that first appeared in these periodicals. The Yale University Library, with great kindness, has allowed me to use its matchless Joyce Collection and to publish material from the manuscripts of *Dubliners* and letters of William Butler Yeats and Ezra Pound, as well as the Duckworth reader's report. The New York Public Library, the National Library in Dublin, the Lockwood Memorial Library at the University of Buffalo, the Houghton Library at Harvard University, and the City College Library in New York have given full co-operation. I wish to acknowledge with gratitude also the kindness of the following publishers in allowing me to use copyright material in this book: The Viking Press, for James Joyce's *Dubliners* (1914), *A Portrait of the Artist as a Young Man* (1916), and *Finnegans Wake* (1939); Random House, Inc., for James Joyce, *Ulysses* (1934); and New Directions, for James Joyce, *Stephen Hero* (1944).

Let me record here, finally, my indebtedness to my students, who each semester surprise me with a fresh, wholesome, and exciting view of Joyce's writings, and to my wife Brenda for unfailing support and inspiration.

M. M.

Contents

I have used footnote references for all citations except those to Joyce's own major works. Page references to the latter are cited in the text, in parentheses, preceded by an identifying letter—for example, (D 107) or (U 625). The key to the letter designations:

D=*Dubliners* (Modern Library)
F=*Finnegans Wake* (The Viking Press)
P=*A Portrait of the Artist as a Young Man* (Modern Library)
S=*Stephen Hero* (New Directions, 1944)
U=*Ulysses* (Modern Library)

The myth of James Joyce as a Stephen Dedalus grown older and wiser is widely accepted, although the acceptance has required a distortion of biographical evidences. Less widespread but equally misleading is the obverse of that view – that the young Joyce was an adolescent version of his mature self, possessing in childhood the full wisdom and craft later displayed in *Ulysses* and in *Finnegans Wake*. Critics are naturally influenced by accounts of the older and nearly blind artist's complete dedication to literature. Impressed by Joyce's own boast that he had put sixteen hundred hours into the composition of but one episode of *Ulysses*, onlookers are awed by the almost hysterical single-mindedness of the middle-aged creator. The maze of consistent interlocking allusions in *Finnegans Wake* emphasizes for them the matchless energy and determination of the man in carrying out whatever literary project he decided to undertake. Fostered partly by the artist himself, the view of Joyce as an inhuman writing machine, a kind of literary Univac incapable of human error, has been gaining ground steadily.

To accept such a stereotyped explanation of Joyce's actions as a mature artist is bad enough; to broaden and lengthen the misconception and apply it to the years of his apprenticeship in Dublin is indefensible. It is possible, of course, for teachers endowed with the certainty that hindsight affords, to describe the logic of development in Joyce's published works. The slight, imitative poetry of *Chamber Music* comes first, followed in logical order by the autobiographical short stories in *Dubliners*, then a more substantial, personal *Portrait*, the great novel *Ulysses*, and finally the shadowy dream language of the *Wake*: an unerring advance from the easy and limited to the complicated and expansive. But the picture of young Joyce, mature in his artistic infancy like Hardy's Little Father Time, will not stand investigation.

There is no question, however, that even at eighteen Joyce knew what he *wanted* to do in literature. Writing admiringly of Ibsen's *When We Dead Awaken* in 1900, he revealed his own artistic ambitions as he evaluated the elder writer's accomplishment.[1] "The subject of Ibsen's play is, in one way, so confined, and, in another way, so vast." The appropriateness of this laudatory commentary needs no elaboration when one considers the story of Mr. Bloom – trivial, vulgar, spanning fewer than twenty-four hours of time; yet on the other hand cosmic, covering symbolically all mankind, from Greek to modern times. *Finnegans Wake* too fits the description: confined to the sleep of one man on one night in Chapelizod, yet it reaches to encompass the collective unconscious of the race and the world's cyclical history.

"Ibsen," says Joyce, "presents his men and women passing through different soul-crises. His analytic method is thus made use of to the fullest extent, and into the comparatively short space of two days the life of all his characters is compressed." The telescoping of time is again iterated and the narrative framework of each of Joyce's books illuminated. Every story in *Dubliners* deals with the supreme moment of comprehension, of spiritual insight or lack of it, in the life of the principal character. The play, *Exiles*, catches Richard Rowan and Bertha at the most pregnant "soul-crisis" of their career. The relationship of Molly and Bloom will never be the same after June 16, 1904. And on the night of *Finnegans Wake* Earwicker's center of familial gravity shifts.

Joyce admires Ibsen, finally, because the Norwegian handles his subject "with large insight, artistic restraint, and sympathy. He sees it steadily and whole, as from a great height, with perfect vision and an angelic dispassionateness." How close Joyce came to approximating this early and idealistic notion of the role of the artist cannot be measured precisely. That he made its fulfillment his task, however, even at this date, is important.

Thrilled by the vastness of Ibsen's canvas and by the universal implications of Hauptmann's *Vor Sonnenaufgang* (*Before Sunrise*) and *Michael Kramer*,[2] the youthful Joyce was fired, like Milton in "Lycidas," to equal or surpass his masters, but in doing this he was going backward rather then forward. Ibsen and Hauptmann have had their day "and the third minister will not be wanting when his hour comes. Even now that hour may be standing by the door."[3] Joyce wrote this elaborate promise when he was nineteen, leaving little doubt that he saw himself in the line of succession. He meant, it may be surmised, that the time was ripe for the artist to spring full-grown from his predecessors – and in the prime of his talent. But, as the neglected record shows, enthusiasm is no substitute for mature artistry.

The result of Joyce's youthful emulation of his masters was

B

an Ibsenesque play, now lost, that apparently tried to solve a good share of the problems of mankind. That this might have been beyond the powers of a teen-ager who had never been out of Ireland is easy to see. Perhaps Joyce was fortunate in selecting William Archer – experienced, wise, and fatherly critic – to give the play its first sensitive reading. Archer's answer, in a letter dated September 15, 1900, is reproduced in full by Stanislaus Joyce in *My Brother's Keeper*. Although Archer did find in Joyce a certain "talent – possibly more than talent," he was puzzled by the meaning of the play and said it was "wildly impossible" for the "commercial stage":

> . . . taking it simply as a dramatic poem, I cannot help finding the canvas too large for the subject. It narrows down in the last act into a sort of love tragedy . . . but in order to reach that point you construct a huge fable of politics & pestilence, in which the reader . . . entirely loses sight of what I presume you intend for the central interest of the drama. I have been trying to read some elaborate symbolism into the second & third acts to account for their gigantic breadth of treatment, but if you had a symbolic purpose, I own it escapes me. . . .[4]

Archer concludes by advising Joyce to "choose a narrower canvas & try to work out a drama with half a dozen clearly designed & vividly projected characters."[5] Almost every one of Archer's critical complaints here reminds one of the barbs hurled with small justice by later critics at Joyce's maturer works.

That Joyce took to heart such strictures as Archer's is clear from his own subsequent opinion on the art of writing. Speaking to Arthur Power, some score of years afterward, he advised his countryman not to seek to model his style on the French satirists. "You will never do it," he said. "You are an Irishman and you must write in your own tradition. Borrowed styles are no good. You must write what is in your blood and not what is in your brain." When Power remonstrated that all great writers are international, Joyce is reported to have replied:

But they were national first . . . and it was the intensity of their own nationalism which made them international in the end, as in the case of Turgenieff. You remember his "Tales of the Sportsman," how local they were – and yet out of that germ he became a great international writer. For myself, I always write about Dublin, because if I can get to the heart of Dublin I can get to the heart of all the cities of the world. In the particular is contained the universal.[6]

Archer's strong indictment of the direction in which Joyce's efforts were tending may well have saved the young artist from wasting any more time on literary material beyond his age and experience.

Nor did Joyce ever resort again to the artificial dramatic embroidery that Archer criticized. None of his stories takes place anywhere but in Ireland, which is also the locale of his play and of his three novels. Instead of the cosmic symbolism that Archer suspected, Joyce turned in later works to symbolic potatoes or mystical cakes of soap. And whatever symbolic analogies he did draw in his major writings were based solidly on universally known touchstones of myth and fable like Homer's *Odyssey* or Dante's representation of Hell. Almost twenty years after Archer's letter Joyce did bring out a "problem" play, *Exiles*. Though like its predecessor it was "wildly impossible" for the "commercial stage," the play did maintain its tight construction as a "love tragedy" throughout. On its "narrower canvas" Joyce was able, as Archer bade, "to work out a drama with half a dozen clearly designed & vividly projected characters." In short, some of the credit that critics have given to Ibsen as an influence on Joyce, the playwright, properly belongs to William Archer.

Joyce was by now striking out in all likely directions with the desperate eagerness born of long frustration. The harsh and narrow social environment of Dublin had no place for a wild apostate without visible means of support. Having rejected the type of economic berth symbolized by the job in Guinness' brewery, as related in *Stephen Hero*, he was confronted with the uncompromising certainty of penury amid the gibes of the Philistines unless he knuckled under or got out.[7] It was not possible to be both a serious writer and a steady eater in the Dublin of 1900. Books and magazines of intellectual stature were seldom published there. London and Paris beckoned as centers of literary activity. Perhaps it would be possible, Joyce thought for a time, to stay at home but publish abroad and thus earn enough to live on. Other considerations, however, made that prospect, even if possible, unattractive.

One attribute that Stephen Dedalus and young Joyce certainly share is loneliness. Stanislaus Joyce speaks of his brother as being unhappy in an unhappy country. Those passages in *Stephen Hero* in which the author describes what it is to have no equal with whom to share one's thoughts and achievements have a depth of autobiographical sincerity that is unquestionable. The protagonist of that book is effectively isolated from all sympathetic understanding and must seek an outlet for his strong feelings in love poetry: "surely it was not wonderful that his solitude should propel him to frenetic outbursts of a young man's passion and to outbursts of loneliness." The unhappy paradox was that, though the solitude was self-imposed, the isolation succeeded in blunting his sense of social responsibility. Worst of all for the young intellectual was his isolation from the world of contemporary letters. Stephen felt himself "living at the farthest remove from the centre of European culture, marooned on an island in the ocean . . . ." Though he despised the lack of literary discernment of those about him at University College and at home, normal pride of authorship made him wish for an audience for his unpublished hymns to beauty. "He kept the manuscript by him and its presence tormented him. He wanted to show it to his parents but . . . he knew that their sympathy would be incomplete. He wanted to show it to Maurice but he was conscious that his brother resented having been forsaken for plebeian companions. He wanted to show it to Lynch." The thought of a lifetime of such isolation was intolerable.[8]

Young Joyce in real life was not much better off. Suspected by his friends for his habit of noting sardonically their pub-crawling activities, he was tolerated as a "character." When he compared the London theater, where he had seen Duse perform in 1900, with the Irish Literary Theatre in Dublin, he vented his disappointment and frustration in his "Day of the Rabblement" pamphlet – surely read by a very limited audience. He showed his verses to A.E., whose puzzlement was ill concealed by a kindly smile.[9] Joyce's sense of isolation was heightened when he perceived that other, lesser artists in Dublin – possibly because they were lesser – had no difficulty in finding favor at the hearth of George Russell or George Moore.[10]

Joyce did not leave Ireland without first trying to make it his base of literary operations. He went through with his plan to address the literary society of University College in 1902, though he knew that his audience would be largely bewildered and hostile. Evidently there was some satisfaction to be gained merely from thinking aloud in the presence of other human beings. Possibly for the meager income but more likely to establish a public link with the literary community in Dublin, Joyce reviewed miscellaneous books for the local newspapers.[11] Such activity apparently did not serve to diminish his loneliness. Nor did the still unexplained rift with his only close friend, J. F. Byrne (Cranly in *A Portrait*), lighten his spirits in 1902. Indigent and confused, the young artist decided to abandon his native city temporarily for the glamor of studying medicine in Paris.

Although most of his friends and advisers – including Archer – took a dim view of the prospect of his combining medical studies with the pursuit of his literary aims, Joyce himself felt an overpowering need to strike out in any direction away from Dublin. Moreover, the record of his activities at the time of his departure shows that he regarded his projected medical career as little more than a convenient excuse. His attention was far more actively directed to warming up irons in the literary fire than to preparing for medical studies. Looking for an easy entry into respectable publishing circles he wrote to Yeats, who advised him:

> I would strongly recommend you to write some little essays. Impressions of books, or better still, of artistic events about you in Paris . . . . You could send some of these at once to the Academy & others later on to the "Speaker." It is always a little troublesome getting ones [*sic*] first start in literature; but after the first start, one can make a pittance if one is industrious, without a great deal of trouble.[12]

In another letter Yeats reported to Joyce that he had tried to find him an editorial post in London, apparently in response to Joyce's plea that Yeats find him a job, but that the editor had not been in. "I am sorry, but for the present you can send some prose to the Academy if you feel an impulse to write. You had better mention my name . . . . I won't give him your little poem, for I gathered from his conversation that he does not like publishing verse, unless it has an obvious look of importance." Yeats goes on to suggest that his young apprentice keep his sheaf of verses for the *Speaker*.[13]

Joyce may have appreciated Yeats's extended advice and generous encouragement, but he seems to have expected, rather arrogantly it would appear, more practical help than words could provide. "I am very sorry," Yeats writes in a later letter, "I cannot help you with money." And he adds, "I did my best to get you work as you know, but that is all I can do for you." [14]

Joyce was systematic in his canvassing of all likely candidates for a grant of funds. He tried his luck with Lady Gregory in 1902, telling her dramatically, in the translated version as it appears in the La Hune Catalogue,

> Je vais me trouver seul, sans amis – on m'a parlé de quelqu'un qui habitait autrefois dans les environs de Montmartre, mais je ne l'ai jamais rencontré – en pays étranger, et je vous écris pour vous demander si vous pouvez m'aider.[15]

[I am going to be alone, without friends – people have told me about someone who used to live in the Montmartre district, but I have never met him – in a foreign country, and I write to you to ask you if you can help me.]

Joyce was to plead in vain, however, for the elderly patroness of letters ignored him.

Joyce's Paris adventure ended suddenly in the middle of 1903 when his mother's death brought him back to Dublin. He had something to show for this brief interlude: a further working out of his ideas on aesthetics, several of the stories of *Dubliners* in early form, and the beginnings of *Stephen Hero*. He had met Europeans and had lived as much as his small means had allowed in the intellectual, bohemian atmosphere of Paris cafés. The discovery that he would fit in, that his talents might be recognized, even though by people who could do nothing for him, must have made the return as bitter as Stephen Dedulus finds it in the "Proteus" episode of *Ulysses*.

First-hand knowledge of what he was missing made the final year in Dublin (1903-4) particularly intolerable. It may account for the frustrated writer's wildness and his fondness for drink, so eagerly recounted by Oliver Gogarty over the years. Sobriety could lead only to impatience with the pallid clique of writers and editors who controlled publication in Ireland. Three stories, paid for at the rate of one pound each, did appear in A.E.'s agricultural newspaper, *The Irish Homestead*, before the venerable sage discovered that they were too formless and inconclusive for the home folks.[16] Joyce presented sections of his autobiographical novel to John Eglinton, the editor of *Dana: A Magazine of Independent Thought*, but again he was rebuffed and his works misunderstood. Gorman tells of the incident in Eglinton's words:

He observed me silently as I read . . . and when I handed it back to him with the timid observation that I did not care to publish what was to myself incomprehensible, he replaced it silently in his pocket.[17]

An unpublished letter from Yeats to Joyce, probably written in 1904, gives evidence that Joyce hoped to earn some money by translating German plays into English for presentation by Yeats' theatre group. Yeats explained that he had given them to a "German scholar to read" and that she had pronounced Joyce "not a very good German scholar." "It is," says Yeats, "very unlikely that we can make any use of them for the theatre." Part of the difficulty was financial, for Yeats hastened to explain that his dramatic organization was at the moment unable to pay for the plays. "Nor do I think it very likely," he continues, "we could attempt German work at present. We must get the ear of our public with Irish work." [18] Whether these translations were of Hauptmann's *Michael Kramer* and *Before Sunrise* – plays which, as noted, had particularly influenced his early thinking – or of other plays by German dramatists is not known. Joyce's translated versions, however, were to remain literary exercises with no chance of presentation in Ireland or elsewhere.

In this year of desperate insecurity, Joyce developed the habit of clutching at economic straws, even at the risk of embarrassing himself and his acquaintances. Suitable positions being scarce, he had his friends on the lookout for small tasks that might keep him in spending money. His former schoolmate Francis Skeffington was able, as registrar of University College, to offer him a few days' employment teaching French at his Alma Mater in 1903. [19] At the same time, "more frequently [for] a matter of shillings than of pounds," he was reviewing books for the *Daily Express* and even reporting the preliminaries to an auto race.

In 1904 Joyce was back on the continent; his life from this time until 1914 has been so well described by Silvio Benco, Herbert Gorman, Stanislaus Joyce, and others that there is no need for extended recapitulation here. [20] A glance at the variety of literary activity occupying his attention during, say, 1906 will show the intensity with which the young artist, in spite of all distractions, attended to his calling. By the middle of February he was sending final versions of the last few stories of *Dubliners* to Grant Richards – "Two Gallants" on February 22, "A Little Cloud" a few weeks later. On February 28 the volume of short stories was accepted by the publisher. March 13 marked the completion of 914 pages, twenty-five chapters, of *Stephen Hero*. During the same year and afterward Joyce's Italian articles on Sinn Fein and other political subjects were in preparation. In June and July he revised "The Sisters," and in August he added three paragraphs to "A Painful Case," slightly annoyed that he would not have time to revise "After the Race" as well. During this time of artistic ferment Joyce was occupied as well by the move to Rome and the adjustment to his new job as a bank clerk, but by October the feverishly busy author bemoaned the fact that his novel was still incomplete, and in the same month he contemplated bringing a suit against Grant Richards. In November, Elkin Mathews accepted *Chamber Music* for publication while Joyce, with almost no time to celebrate the long-overdue event, planned his *novella* "The Dead." In spite of the time consumed by all these activities Joyce managed to spend the autumn months reading extensively in Wilde, George Moore, Hauptmann, Gissing, Maupassant, and Anatole France. The year 1906 saw, finally, the dim beginnings of *Ulysses*.[21]

It is paradoxical that Joyce should have strained every creative fiber for the delectation of a public so ill equipped to appreciate or even to understand what he was doing. Granted that the immediate aftermath of the Oscar Wilde fiasco at the turn of the century had frightened both public and publishers into meek acceptance of insipid modes in writing, it is scarcely to be expected that, as late as 1915, half a generation later, major British publishers should be rejecting *A Portrait* because it was "naughty" or because its author was a "very young" man.[22] An interesting and reliable index to both lay and professional tastes during Joyce's apprenticeship is the reader's report on *A Portrait* submitted to the publishing firm of Duckworth & Company by an anonymous adviser, possibly Edward Garnett. The report shows sensitive insights along traditional lines but falls down in mistaking the short cuts of impressionism for uncraftsmanlike confusion. The entire report follows:

James Joyce's "Portrait of the Artist as a Young Man" wants going through carefully from start to finish. There are many 'longueurs.' Passages which, though the publisher's reader may find them entertaining, will be tedious to the ordinary man among the reading public. That public will call the book, as it stands at present, realistic, unprepossessing, unattractive. We call it ably written. The picture is 'curious,' it arouses interest and attention. But the author must revise it and let us see it again. It is too discursive, formless, unrestrained, and ugly things, ugly words, are too prominent; indeed at times they seem to be shoved in one's face, on purpose, unnecessarily. The point of view will be voted 'a little sordid.' The picture of life is good; the period well brought to the reader's eye, and the types and characters are well drawn, but it is too 'unconventional.' This would stand against it in normal times. At the present time, though the old conventions are in the background, we can only see a chance for it if it is pulled into shape and made more definite.

In the earlier portion of the Ms. as submitted to us, a good deal of pruning can be done. Unless the author will use restraint and proportion he will not gain readers. His pen and his thoughts seem to have run away with him sometimes.

At the end of the book there is a complete falling to bits; the pieces of writing and the thoughts are all in pieces and they fall like damp, ineffective rockets.

The author shows us he has art, strength and originality, but this Ms. wants time and trouble spent on it, to make it a more finished piece of work, to shape it more carefully as the product of the craftsmanship, mind and imagination of an artist.[23]

On December 3, 1915, the Duckworth firm communicated the gist of its reader's conclusions, using frequent quotations from his report, to Joyce's agent, James B. Pinker. Realizing the unpleasantness involved in telling a novelist of Joyce's stamp that he must correct his alleged sloppiness in order to qualify for a place on the publisher's list, Pinker sought to enlist the good offices of Ezra Pound as mediator. Joyce already had reason to know of Pound's high opinion of his work and might be swayed to revise *A Portrait* if its faults were enumerated by so erudite and enthusiastic a friend. But Pinker had not counted on the vehemence of the fiery editor's emotions, made clear to him in an explosive letter hitherto unpublished:

I have read the effusion of Mr. Duckworth's reader with no inconsiderable disgust. These vermin crawl over and beslime our literature with their pulings, and nothing but the day of judgement can, I suppose, exterminate 'em. Thank god one need not under ordinary circumstances touch them.

Hark to his puling squeek.

too 'unconventional'. What in hell do we want but some change from the unbearable monotony of the weekly six shilling pears soap annual novel . . . .

'Carelessly written', this of the sole, or almost sole piece of contemporary prose that one can enjoy sentence by sentence and reread with pleasure . . . .

It is with difficulty that I manage to write to you at all on being presented with the Duckworthian'muck, the dungminded, dung-beard, penny-a line, please-the-mediocre-at-all-cost doctrine. You English will get no prose till you exterminate this breed . . . .

to say nothing of the abominable insolence of the tone . . . .

I must repeat my former offer, if this louse will specify exactly what verbal changes he wants made I will approach Joyce in the matter. But I most emphatically will not forward the insults of an imbecile to one of the very few men for whom I have the faintest respect.

Canting supercilious blockhead . . . . I always sup[p]osed from report that Duckworth was an educated man, but I can not reconcile this opinion with his retention of the author of the missive you sent me . . . .

God. 'a more finished piece of work' . . . .

And the end . . [*sic*] also found fault with . . . again, **Oh, God, O Montreal** . . . .

> Why can't you send the publishers readers to the serbian front, and get some good out of the war . . . .
>
> Serious writers will certainly give up the use of english altogether unless you can improve the process of publication . . . .
>
> [handwritten at the end of letter] They pour out Elinor Glynn [*sic*] & pornography after pornography but a piece of good writing they hate. I am reminded that Landor had equal difficulty in getting published – yet he is the best mind in your literature.
>
> as for altering Joyce to suit Duckworth's reader – i[t] would [be] like trying to fit the Venus de Milo into a pisspot – a few changes required.[24]

It goes without saying that the suggested revisions were never made, possibly because a more enterprising publisher in the United States decided to bring out Joyce's text as it stood. Remarkable as the Pound–Pinker exchange was, it simply epitomized Joyce's constant difficulties with recalcitrant publishers before the notoriety of *Ulysses* made him a valuable property. The wonder is that he managed to plan and execute his literary contributions so carefully and devotedly, always with the nagging doubt in his mind that they would ever get into print.

In his book about his famous brother, Stanislaus Joyce insists that Joyce had "a fixed objection to altering anything he had published." This may be so, but it is obvious from the several drafts of certain stories of *Dubliners*, worked on after the stories had appeared in the *Irish Homestead*, that Joyce was capable of overcoming this objection in the interest of a better literary product. Also, the fact that episodes of *Ulysses* and *Finnegans Wake* appear in several published versions makes Stanislaus's generalization suspect.[25]

Care and devotion are apparent in all Joyce's books – even in preliminary drafts and notebook jottings. He might change his mind about a sentence or a paragraph once he had written it, but not because his first attempt had been frivolous or capricious. Second thought might find a better way to put his idea; it would not change the serious, single-minded aim with which the original version had been penned. A critic who deals with the writings of an artist like Joyce finds it especially valuable, therefore, to look not only at the final product, the published work, but also at the significant steps along the way. The path from notebook jotting through full first draft to finished book is strewn with meaningful clues to the author's thought and artistry. The early works make an exciting study in themselves, especially when the critic is able to examine successive stages in their development. They are equally fascinating to study for the insights they provide into Joyce's later art, for occasionally the glimmerings of a Leopold Bloom or a motif of the *Wake* flicker faintly in a manuscript note of the 1890s.[26]

Joyce's scribbled "epiphanies" of this period – notebook jottings, few of them more than one hundred words long, capturing a few lines of conversation, a passing observation, a commonplace occurrence lifted suddenly to a plane of heightened significance – illustrate his early concern with materials and episodes later to be incorporated into his more ambitious productions.[27] One such is a brief description of a scene involving two small children and a beggar whom they have been baiting. The derelict threatens to cut out the livers and "lights" (lungs) of both children, meanwhile menacing them with his stick. The scene fades out as suddenly as it appeared – as swiftly as it would disappear in real life when the passing observer continued his stroll beyond the point of action. Another and apparently unrelated epiphany is a dramatized version of an invasion of the Joyce home by a Mr. Vance whose stick threatens the small boy, James Joyce, and whose attitude evokes, in its earliest known appearance, the awful refrain

> Pull out his eyes,
> Apologise,
> Apologise,
> Pull out his eyes. (P 2)

The general outlines of the motif as it appears in *A Portrait* have been examined extensively and need only be recalled here. Stephen hides under the table while his mother and his nurse repeat the menacing verse. The presence on the same page of the information that the small boy is going to marry the Protestant Eileen when they grow up suggests that religious and sexual guilt have motivated his concealment, and, by extension, the vague threats of his authoritarian elders. Hugh Kenner suggests the presence of the Promethean crime (stealing fire from the Gods) and punishment (having eagles eternally pluck at his self-replenishing liver), but he is unable to demonstrate any definite intent on the part of the artist to involve Prometheus.[28] Substitution of eyes for liver, of course, is easily accounted for by Joyce's personal difficulties, even as a child, with his sight.

With the background of the extant epiphanies, however, it is possible to see how Joyce arrives at the end-product presented on page 2 of *A Portrait*. In the first notebook jotting the adult figure with a stick threatens vulgarly both liver and lights of the terrified children. Though Joyce must have known that "lights" commonly signified "lungs," figurative use of the word to connote "eyes" was an easy and logical artistic step. It is probable that Joyce actually was witness to just such a scene as he describes, for according to the testimony of those who knew him well when he was collecting his epiphanies, as well as according to his own evidence, none of these raw materials for literature was artificially manufactured. It is safe to conclude, too, that when he recorded it he had no thought that it would eventually find a place in his *Portrait* – and certainly none that it would come to bear overtones of the Prometheus myth. The second epiphany – Mr. Vance entering the small boy's home, stick in hand, to threaten him, presumably for a childish infraction – must have struck its recorder as basically like the earlier one. Again authority in a menacing attitude, again the frightened and confused child, again the weapon and the threat of bodily harm. This time, however, the fundamental situation must be more than merely recorded: it must be fashioned into the stuff of controlled, imaginative fiction. The beggar and Mr. Vance merge, obviously enough, to become a fused symbol of authority – the parent-nurse of the small boy in the novel. The two children of the beggar epiphany merge with the small James Joyce of the Mr. Vance epiphany to become Stephen Dedalus – Joyce's symbol of beleaguered artists everywhere, condemned by menacing outsiders for vague crimes against society. At this point of imaginative reconstruction Joyce may well have seen the double implication that remained, for the taking, in the imprecation of the beggar. Stephen-Prometheus-Joyce might now be the culmination of the two rough and discrete epiphanies, dependent on both for existence, but greater in significance than either.

By reference to the same epiphany jottings the critic can also construct a progression from the impersonally observed event, through the strictly personal application in the Mr. Vance episode (the boy's name there is "Joyce" and Mr. Vance was a neighbour of the Joyces at Bray), to the proper evocation of distance in autobiographical fiction – the stage in which Joyce has become Stephen and the plight of the boy is broadened to give symbolic depth to the flat story of a middle-class Dubliner.

Joyce's rich and complex writing needs, then, to be looked at against as wide a background as possible of the writer's early attempts at story-telling. The omissions are as meaningful often as the additions to the early versions, the alterations as significant as the passages which are allowed to stand unchanged. Only by close study of a cross section of Joyce's early fiction and its evolving pattern can an approach be made to the remarkable mind that created the later work.

In his classic study of the way Coleridge's reading shaped his creative imagination, John Livingston Lowes finds that "Coleridge . . . read with an eye which habitually pierced to the secret spring of poetry beneath the crust of fact." [1] Lowes reports further that Coleridge's curious insistence on following up every lead which a book might offer "makes it possible to follow him into the most remote and unsuspected fields." Though Joyce in contemporary literature probably comes closest to the encyclopedic depth of his predecessor in the extent and the outlandishness of his reading, the Irish author's use of what he read in creating his own fiction differs considerably from Coleridge's. Joyce seems less anxious to touch "the secret spring of poetry" than to acquire practical information concerning obscure happenings of history or myth. Moreover, while Coleridge was apparently delighted and surprised to find corroborative embroidery for his poetry by the merest chance, Joyce carefully planned his schedule of reading to track down the factual information which his literary project of the moment demanded. His letters to his relatives, and to friends like Frank Budgen and Harriet Weaver, are filled with requests for books on the occult, on the Greeks, and on the topography of distant cities.

When he was not reading to discover informational details for inclusion in a specific story or novel, Joyce seems to have been impressed mainly, both as impersonal artist and supreme egotist, by analogies to his own life and to the books he himself was planning. If the mere fact that James Stephens had the same birthday as he had could have thrilled the mature Joyce, it is no wonder that discovering Ibsen to be, like himself, a social outcast, vigorous anti-Philistine, and rebel in literary style and subject matter, kindled within the young Irishman a bright flame of kinship. No wonder, too, that with his own weak eyes, with his decision to be a wanderer and exile and singer of bitter songs, he might find the analogy of Homer especially welcome and even, one day, try his hand at a modern *Odyssey*. Kinship with his literary heroes – biographically, psychologically, artistically – seems to have been a necessity for the artist as a *young* man, less important once he himself had become the literary hero of a newer generation. But by this latter day, Joyce had only one major work left to write. In terms of developmental influences, therefore, it is Joyce as he was in the days when he wore the mask of Stephen Dedalus who demands attention.

Once Joyce had adopted for his hero worship any literary god, he extracted in full measure whatever such a figure might have to offer. The young author of *A Portrait* seems thus to have appropriated from James Mangan, for use during

C

the next thirty-eight years of his creative efforts, not alone Mangan's personal history, but, in addition, his account of his father and his associates, his poetry, his nationalism, and even the very figures of speech which Mangan had used to describe his unhappy lot. When it came to writing, Joyce had a practical eye: he could see instantly as he read a book how it might be turned to account, totally, perhaps, through a contemporary parody of its episodes (*The Divine Comedy* superimposed upon the short story "Grace"); partially, through the adaptation of the idea behind Vico's theory of history as a way of giving order to the confusion of the *Wake*.

Many people have supplied what information they have had concerning Joyce's opinions of the books he was reading. Stanislaus Joyce, in his *Recollections*, offers a useful and interesting list. Padraic Colum contributes helpful memories as do others who were intimate with the author during his long, formative period. The most elaborate work on Joyce's private library – of limited importance to students of the early Joyce but excellent as a means of understanding the catholicity of taste of the middle-aged artist – is *The Personal Library of James Joyce: A Descriptive Bibliography*, prepared by Thomas E. Connolly at the University of Buffalo.[2] Other studies certainly will follow. By examining a few illustrations of Joyce's technique of borrowing, I hope to show how he usually made use of several literary sources to produce literature of a high order. Obviously, any author is influenced by what he has read; even forty years ago T. S. Eliot knew that he was perpetuating a cliché in saying so, but in the case of such eclectic writers as Pound and Eliot and Joyce, this axiom is supremely true. They are concerned not merely with the general ideas and techniques of their predecessors, but with their very lines and words, which they reconstruct in a new mosaic of verbal power. To paraphrase a contemporary critic, "Immature artists borrow; mature artists steal"; and Joyce was a mature artist.

One of the most powerful stories in *Dubliners* is "A Painful

Case." Much of its strength lies in its deep concern with two basic human experiences, love and death. Yet Joyce seems somehow less concerned with these in themselves than with the personality of his main character, James Duffy. The author's intense analysis of the intellectual and emotional life of this protagonist suggests that Joyce himself is Mr. Duffy. Events in the author's life are seemingly paralleled by occurrences in Duffy's life. Both men enjoy, and yet suffer from, the exile which they have imposed upon themselves: "Duffy . . . wished to live as far as possible from the city of which he was a citizen" (D 133). Mr. Duffy, like Joyce, lacks "friends, church . . . creed. He lived his spiritual life without any communion with others" (D 135). The hero of "A Painful Case" scornfully refuses to "compete with phrasemongers" or "submit himself to the criticisms of an obtuse middle class" (D 138). And Joyce's years-long war with the British printer over the publication of *Dubliners* was fought over just this principle.[3] The author's remarks about Shem in *Finnegans Wake* show how long his bitterness with Philistine standards of art and morality was to last.[4] "The soul's incurable loneliness" (D 139) recalls passages on a similar theme in the autobiographical *Portrait of the Artist*.[5] Duffy's despair as he observes "venal and furtive loves" (D 146) which he cannot share may be likened to Stephen Dedalus' feelings in *Ulysses*[6] and then translated into the emotions of Joyce in his hard, early years of exile from Ireland.

As well, by the inclusion of certain items of information in his story, the author shows a similarity of temperament and intellectual interests between Duffy and himself. "In the desk," Joyce writes, "lay a manuscript translation of Hauptmann's *Michael Kramer* . . . and a little sheaf of papers held together by a brass pin. In these sheets a sentence was inscribed from time to time" (D 134). This naming of the same play which, according to Herbert Gorman,[7] Joyce had also admired and translated in his youth is more than accidental. The little sheaf of papers, moreover, suggests the notebook jottings of the author, perhaps even the scribbling of epiphanies. "He never gave alms to beggars and walked firmly, carrying a stout hazel" (D 135). Duffy's only entertainment, his love of opera or concert, recalls Joyce's lifelong interest in these arts as diversion from daily worries.

In his attitude toward physical love, however, Joyce's literary counterpart, Stephen Dedalus, is in only partial agreement with Mr. Duffy. The ostensibly autobiographical work, *Stephen Hero*, reveals Stephen confessing a "longing for a mad night of love . . . a desperate willingness to cast his soul away, his life and his art, and to bury them all with her under fathoms of «lust-laden» slumber." [8] This surely is a far cry from Mr. Duffy's intention. That Stephen does not realize his desire is the fault sometimes of his adolescent uncertainty and fumbling in the face of strong emotion, sometimes of the unwillingness of his female companion to acquiesce in so ambitious an enterprise. But on those occasions when the opportunity for physical love seems almost thrust upon him, as in this dialogue between Stephen and Emma Clery, he fails to take advantage of his chances:

– But you are not a man, are you? she said quickly for pride and youth and desire were beginning to inflame her cheek . . . .
– I am a hobbledehoy, said Stephen.
She leaned a little more towards him . . . . The warmth of her body seemed to flow into his and without a moment's hesitation he put his hand into his pocket and began to finger out his coins.
– I must be going in, she said.
– Goodnight . . . (S 189)

When one compares this incident with the crucial event in "A Painful Case," Duffy's rejection of the love of Mrs. Sinico, one may feel that here is at least a partial parallel. "He thought that in her eyes he would ascend to an angelical stature; and . . . he heard the strange impersonal voice which he recognised as his own, insisting on the soul's incurable loneliness. We cannot give ourselves, it said; we are our own. The end of these discourses was that one night . . . Mrs. Sinico caught up his hand passionately" (D 138-139). The resemblance is merely superficial, however, for, though Stephen's withdrawal is involuntary and painful, Duffy, with conscious intellectual precision, coldly rejects the advances of his companion.

The time of writing and the circumstances under which the story was written offer further evidence that Mr. Duffy should not be regarded as a strictly autobiographical figure, in spite of many parallels. One draft of "A Painful Case," in most respects identical with the final published version, is dated in Joyce's hand "15-8-05." [9] By this time, the author had settled down to as ordinary a life of devoted husband as a struggling genius can have.[10] He had not impulsively whisked young Nora Barnacle away from Ireland because of the intellectual stimulation she afforded.[11] Those who knew the Joyces on the Continent, no matter how biting their evaluation of the author as a man or artist may be, concur in their opinion that he seemed the ideal *paterfamilias* and a faithful, loving husband.[12] If these evidences may be credited, then the writer of the stories emerges as a man basically very different from his emotionally disturbed and distorted protagonist, certainly not one in need of the comfort that some writers derive from projecting their marital difficulties into their writings.[13]

In considering the character of Mr. Duffy, one must recall too, Joyce's rigorous attention to the inclusion of only those details which contribute materially to a fuller understanding of his story. His identification of several of the books on Duffy's bookshelves is thus neither random nor superfluous. By this means Joyce offers the broad hint that part of Mr. Duffy's character is molded from observations made by Nietzsche in *Thus Spake Zarathustra*. Nietzsche's remarks on womankind show that autobiography is subordinated to the use of a literary source in Joyce's presentation of Mr. Duffy. Is this not Duffy speaking?

Allzulange war im Weibe ein Sklave und ein Tyrann versteckt. Deshalb ist das Weib noch nicht der Freundschaft fähig: es kennt nur die Liebe . . . . Und auch in der wissenden Liebe des Weibes ist immer noch Überfall und Blitz und Nacht neben dem Lichte.

Noch ist das Weib´nicht der Freundschaft fähig: Katzen sind immer noch die Weiber, und Vögel. Oder, besten Falles, Kühe.[14]

[Too long have a slave and a tyrant lain hid in woman. Therefore is woman not yet capable of friendship: she knoweth only love . . . . And even where woman loveth with knowledge there is ever, with the light, surprise and lightning and night.

As yet woman is not capable of friendship: women are yet ever cats and birds. Or, at the best, cows.]*

Recall the sentence written in Mr. Duffy's notebook: "Love between man and man is impossible because there must not be sexual intercourse, and friendship between man and woman is impossible because there must be sexual intercourse" (D 140). Nietzsche exhorts a man of Duffy's type: "Und hüte dich auch vor den Anfällen deiner Liebe! Zu schnell streckt der Einsame dem die Hand entgegen, der ihm begegnet." [15] ["Beware the assaults of thy love! Too readily doth the solitary stretch out his hand to him that meeteth with him."]

Joyce relies upon Nietzsche for a great deal more than his remarks on woman. He uses Nietzsche's idea of the superman, and makes it, in fact, the basis of the character of Duffy. Master of his mind and his emotions in the well-ordered life which he has made for himself, Duffy appears satisfied with a solitary, self-sufficient existence. For the herd he has only scorn; for the weak, even for Mrs. Sinico, only a kind of disgust. This is also the attitude of the superman. Says Nietzsche: "Das Leben ist ein Born der Lust; aber wo das Gesindel mit trinkt, da sind alle Brunnen vergiftet." He continues sadly:

---

* Note: All English translations of Nietzsche's *Zarathustra* are by A. Tille, from the J. M. Dent & Sons edition (London, 1933).

"Und mancher, der sich vom Leben abkehrte, kehrte sich nur vom Gesindel ab." [16] ["Life is a wellspring of delight; but wheresoever the rabble drink all wells are poisoned . . . . And many an one that hath turned from life hath turned only from the rabble."]
Duffy, like the superman, renounces his creed and has no friends. He is particularly disgusted with matters of the market place, willing for a short time to be intellectual leader of a small workingman's political group, but quick to quit the movement when he is forced to share the leadership. He might have admitted his error in the words of Zarathustra: "Als ich zum ersten Male zu den Menschen kam, da tat ich die Einsiedler-Torheit . . . ich stellte mich auf den Markt. Und als ich zu allen redete, redete ich zu keinem." Nietzsche's superman also discovers his own mistake: "Mit dem neuen Morgen aber kam mir eine neue Wahrheit . . . : 'Was geht mich Markt und Pöbel und Pöbel-Lärm und lange Pöbel-Ohren an!' " [17] ["When for the first time I went unto men, I committed the hermit-folly . . . I stood in the market place. And in that I spake to all I spake to none. But with the new morning a new truth came unto me . . . . What care I for the market place and the mob and the mob's clamour!"] Duffy resorts to this same argument when he is asked why he does not publish his reflections. He is violent in his ridicule of the critical opinions of the rabble, the "obtuse middle class which entrusted its morality to policemen and its fine arts to impresarios" (D 138), for "übel riecht alles Gestern und Heute nach dem schreibenden Gesindel." [18] ["all to-day stinketh of the scribbling rabble."]

Feeling himself far above the rabble, Mr. Duffy, Dublin's Higher Man, firmly expects to "ascend to an angelical stature" in the eyes of his weaker companion. Being a mere mortal, Mrs. Sinico is not fit to survive the shock of his rebuff. In her degradation and death, however, are the seeds of his own downfall, for slowly the realization of the enormity of his actions succeeds in breaking down the whole moral, or amoral, structure about which his life is built, and he is left merely a lonesome, ineffectual human being. "Der Mann fürchte sich vor dem Weibe," says the sage, "wenn es liebt: da bringt es jedes Opfer, und jedes andre Ding gilt ihm ohne Wert." [19] ["Let man fear woman . . . when she loveth: then will she sacrifice all, and naught else hath value for her."]

The "painful" case actually is not the accidental death of Mrs. Sinico but the morbidly dreary life of a man who has shut out all love from his life, deliberately and cold-bloodedly, in a mistaken attempt to channelize and categorize emotion just as he has arranged books neatly on bookshelves, just as he has observed a strict routine in his eating habits. It is the case of a man emotionally dead – and dead of his own volition. For the hour of realization, Joyce sets the stage carefully. Duffy wanders into a public house alone and sits down opposite "five or six workingmen," representatives of the rabble once so distasteful to him. They smoke, spit, wear heavy boots, are "vulgar." Yet they are happy, normal people, sitting apart from him, probably suspicious of him. In this setting, he feels what is probably the first remorse of his life, though he still seeks to excuse his despicable actions and thoughts. The will to power, he finds, does not necessarily lead to happiness; nor can a ruthless celibacy and Spartan abstinence compensate for a lack of basic humanity.

Joyce's careful working in of Nietzsche's prescription for a superman, without which Mr. Duffy would undoubtedly have emerged a very different kind of person, helps to show the danger of too close identification of Joyce's heroes with himself. Even more revealing, along this same line, is his debt to Gerhart Hauptmann.

When Hauptmann's *Michael Kramer* was published in 1900, Joyce was mightily impressed with it, and even took the trouble to translate it into English. [20] What impressed him most, perhaps, was its skillful blend of naturalism and symbolism – something which the young Irishman was trying to perfect in his own work. Certainly he must have been impressed by the story of uncompromising artistic integrity represented by the painter, Michael Kramer, beset on all sides by Philistinism, incompetence, and mediocrity; and utterly quelled at the last by the death of his son, which wakens all the latent emotion in him and calls forth an impassioned speech on the smallness of everyday concerns beside the finality of death. Joyce was not one to let so powerful a situation go untapped.

The irony of Mr. Duffy's translating Hauptmann's play is that in doing so he is given first a picture of himself and of his barren life, and then he is shown the tragedy that must inevitably result from such a course of emotionless perfection. That he fails to heed Hauptmann's words and thus suffers almost the same pangs as Michael Kramer supplies an added touch of irony.

The specific parallels between the two literary works merit examination. Both Duffy and Kramer are artists isolated from the communities in which they live by their uncompromising hatred of the rabble. It is said of Kramer that he helps his pupils by knocking the Philistinism out of them.[21] Both men abhor "anything which betokened physical or mental disorder" (D 134). Joyce's description of Duffy's room and Hauptmann's stage directions for the furnishing of Kramer's studio are remarkably similar. Joyce stresses the plain, bare cleanliness and meticulous order of the room: ". . . four cane chairs, a clothes-rack . . . a square table on which lay a double desk . . . . The books on the white wooden shelves were arranged from below upwards according to bulk" (D 133). Kramer's studio contains old furniture, "ein kleines Tischchen" ["a small table"] used as a desk, "Zwei einfache Rohrstühle . . . . Es herrscht überall Sauberkeit und peinliche Ordnung." ["simple cane chairs . . . . cleanliness and the nicest order predominate."] One of Kramer's first actions on stage is significant: "Er steht auf . . . dann fängt er an, die gestörte Ordnung auf seinem Tischchen wieder herzustellen." [22] ["He stands up . . . then he sets about restoring the disturbed order of his little table."] *

What may be accidental similarities in the physical description of the two protagonists can be passed over in favor of the more significant parallels in the remarks of both men on their environment. Mr. Duffy's opinion of public taste and the literary discernment of the average man has been recorded. His counterpart, Kramer, likewise bemoans the fact that the mediocre in ability and intelligence are in key positions and "So müssen die Besten beiseite stehn." [23] Like Duffy, he defends himself against such a· public of dolts by isolation. He refuses to display his paintings: "Das Eigne, das Echte, Tiefe und Kräftige, das wird nur in Einsiedeleien geboren. Der Künstler ist immer der wahre Einsiedler." ["The original, the genuine, the deep and strong in art grows only in a hermitage – is born only in utter solitude. The artist is always the true hermit."]

Like Milton, in a way, and Joyce, and Duffy, Kramer believes that if a man wants to paint Christ, for instance, he needs "kein Leben in Saus und Braus: Einsame Stunden, einsame Tage, einsame Jahre, sehn Se 'mal an." The artist, he explains, must "mit sich allein sein, mit seinem Leiden und seimen Gott . . . . Nichts Gemeines darf an ihm und in ihm sein . . . . Da sieht man den Heiland!" [24] ["a lifetime . . . not . . . of revelry or noise, but lonely hours, lonely days, lonely years . . . . [The artist, he explains] must be alone with his sorrow and with his God . . . . Nothing low or mean must be about him or within him . . . . You see the Saviour then . . . ."] The distortion of this idea in Duffy's mind makes his untenable position with Mrs. Sinico seem, to him, completely justified.

All these similarities are minor, however, before the likenesses in the climactic scenes of both works. Through his

* Note: All English translations of *Michael Kramer* are by Ludwig Lewisohn, in the B. W. Heubsch edition of *The Dramatic Works of Gerhart Hauptmann*, vol. 3 (New York, 1922).

inability to understand his son, whom he really loves, Kramer goads the ugly, crippled, morally inferior youth to suicide. While Arnold is yet alive, his character gives Michael Kramer an opportunity to expand on the subject of vulgarity: "Hör'n Se, ich könnte alles verzeihn, aber Gemeinheit verzeih' ich nicht. Eine niedrige Seele widert mich an, und sehn Se, die hat er." [25] ["I can forgive anything, but I can't forgive the . . . ignoble. A vulgar soul revolts me, and that's what he has . . . ."] Duffy expresses the same feelings towards Mrs. Sinico in his belief that "the details of a commonplace vulgar death attacked his stomach. Not merely had she degraded herself; she had degraded him" (D 144). But Arnold's death brings his father up sharply. Kramer's long speech at the end and Duffy's final thoughts are strikingly alike. Both find that the precise and orderly way of life in matters of detail does not compensate for the fact of death, which sweeps aside all lesser matters. Hauptmann puts it this way:

> Wenn erst das Grosse ins Leben tritt, hör'n Se, dann ist alles Kleine wie weggefegt. Das Kleine trennt, das Grosse, das eint, sehn Se. Das heisst, man muss so geartet sein. Der Tod ist immer das Grosse, hör'n Se: der Tod und die Liebe, sehn Se mal an. . . . .
> So was will einem erst gar nicht in den Kopf. Nun sitzt es. Nun lebt man schon wieder damit. Nun ist er schon bald zwei Tage dahin. Ich war die Hülse, dort liegt der Kern. Hätten sie doch die Hülse genommen!
> Da lebt man so hin: das muss alles so sein! Man schlägt sich mit kleinen Sachen herum, und hör'n Se, man nimmt sie wer weiss wie wichtig, man macht sich Sorgen, man ächzt, und man klagt, und hör'n Se, dann kommt das mit einem mal . . . da heisst es: Posto gefasst! [26]

> [When the great things enter into our lives . . . the trivial things are suddenly swept away. The trivial separates . . . but greatness unites us . . . . And death . . . always belongs to the great things – death and love.
> A thing like this [death] – we can't grasp it at first. Now it's entered the mind. Now it's become part of life. It's almost two

days ago now. I was the shell; there lies the kernel. If only the shell had been taken!

We live along, take our accustomed ways for granted, worry over small affairs, think ourselves and our little annoyances mightily important . . . . And then, suddenly, a thing of this kind comes down upon us . . . . Then . . . it is hard to stand one's ground.]

Then feelings of remorse come to increase the misery of the living: "Das ganze Leben lang war ich sein Schulmeister. Ich habe den Jungen malträtiert . . . . Ich hab' diese Pflanze vielleicht erstickt. Vielleicht hab' ich ihm seine Sonne verstellt: dann wär' er in meinem Schatten verschmachtet . . . . Aber ich bin zusammengeschrumpft. Ich bin ganz erbärmlich vor ihm geworden." ["All his life long I was his schoolmaster. I had to maltreat him . . . . Perhaps I smothered this plant. Perhaps I shut out his sun and he perished in my shadow . . . . I have shrivelled into nothingness. I have become a wretched creature beside him . . . ."] The summing up, all passion spent, is quiet: "Die Liebe, sagt man, ist stark wie der Tod. Aber kehren Se getrost den Satz mal um: Der Tod ist auch mild wie die Liebe . . . der Tod ist verleumdet worden." [27] ["Love, it is said, is strong as death. But you may confidently reverse the saying: Death is as gentle as love . . . death has been maligned."]

At first word of the death of Mrs. Sinico, Duffy is overwhelmed by self-pity and disgust at having known such an unworthy person. He "can't grasp" the finality of her act right away. Then, as Kramer says, her death becomes part of life and he "thought her hand touched his." Remorse enters here, as above, and he "asked himself what else could he have done . . . . He had done what seemed to him best." Now, as never before, he is able to see her side of the story, as Kramer begins to see Arnold's side. "Now that she was gone he understood how lonely her life must have been, sitting night after night alone in that room" (D 144-145). And suddenly Duffy sees the loneliness of his own life, seems ready, in fact, to cry out in Michaline Kramer's words, "Aber überleben, das ist wohl das Schwerste." [". . . to survive at all! That, surely, is hardest."] [28] Kramer's image of shutting out Arnold's sun is paralleled by Duffy's fear that he had "denied her life and happiness: he had sentenced her to ignominy, a death of shame" (D 146). It has not been pointed out before that this play, which Mr. Duffy gives such care to, even writing the stage directions "in purple ink," contains the entire moral fable that Duffy needs in order to change his ways and live a normal, wholesome life. Surely Joyce was conscious of this irony when he introduced *Michael Kramer* into his own story.

Joyce's brother Stanislaus adds still another dimension to the figure of James Duffy. He insists that "A Painful Case" is "an imaginary portrait of what my brother thought I should become in middle age." Stanislaus tells of his own chance meeting with the woman whom Joyce calls Mrs. Sinico - "an unknown lady" - and claims that the details of her personal life were fabricated by the author. Even Duffy's epigrams were borrowed, Stanislaus says, from a sheaf of papers on which he himself used to take notes. Joyce's brother does concede that, "in order to raise Mr. Duffy's cultural standard he [Joyce] . . . introduced a few traits taken from his own life, such as the translation of *Michael Kramer* and mention of Nietzsche, who interested me hardly at all, but he drew little from himself because he had reason not to consider himself a good type of celibate." [29] Though Stanislaus has always displayed a marked willingness to identify himself with most of Joyce's work, as helper, adviser, and even as semi-fictional character, it is not hard to believe that, in this instance, the young author did indeed add some of his brother's contributions to autobiography and to borrowing from literary sources.

It is difficult to point as definitely to borrowing from Hauptmann's *Before Sunrise* (*Vor Sonnenaufgang*), but the Irishman's lifelong enthusiasm for the play undoubtedly had its effect and deserves at least passing mention. The Slocum-Cahoon

Bibliography shows to what extent young Joyce was committed to the play, for he translated all twenty-four thousand words of it into English – a task which took the better part of the summer of 1901. In October of that year, at the age of nineteen, he was to designate Hauptmann the "successor" of Ibsen in "The Day of the Rabblement." Thirty-six years later, his hero worship unabated, he was to write Ezra Pound, asking: "Could you give me a word of introduction to Gerhart Hauptmann! When I was a boy in Dublin I made a translation (!) of his . . . play which I still admire greatly. Perhaps he would do me the honour and pleasure of signing it – his text I mean, not my well meant translation . . . ." [30] It would be surprising if such long-term devotion had not left marks on Joyce's own production.

Before Sunrise, first performed in Germany in 1889, depicts the revolting conditions under which the *nouveau riche* peasants of the Silesian coal districts live their lives. [31] Like Ibsen's dramas, this play is heavy, drab, at times melodramatic, pregnant with the blasted fruits of a cursed heredity, and, to a contemporary reader, lacking sufficiently in motivation and inevitability to make the dramatic intensity believable. Except in parody, Joyce could not have written anything using its plot and design. What the young apprentice did seize upon, however, was the characterization. As he had done in the works of Mangan and Bulwer-Lytton, he appropriated those characters and situations within the general story which might serve as analogies and surrogates, literary substitutes for the people and scenes of his own projected narratives.

Hauptmann's play contained for Joyce an early dramatic objectification of the character of Stephen Dedalus, of Shem and Shaun, and of a type epitomized by Mr. Duffy and Gabriel Conroy. In the characterization of most of these personalities, too, there lurks the figure of James Joyce, the artist as a young man. Such a combination would have been too much for the Irish student to resist.

Almost at the beginning of the play the audience is told of Frederick Hildebrandt, an artist whose life has ended in suicide. He had modeled statues which the vulgar public had not understood and had not liked because they were not entertaining to look at. Hildebrandt had entered an art contest, nonetheless, won the prize, and then killed himself. For Joyce, the moral of this vignette would probably have been that the true artist "abhors the multitude." He goes on, in "The Day of the Rabblement": " . . . the artist, though he may employ the crowd, is very careful to isolate himself." Yet, Joyce finds in the Ireland of 1901, "it is strange to see the artist making terms with the rabblement." [32] The Irish Literary Theatre, by trying to please the public, to win general favor, is committing suicide. Michael Kramer, at great cost to his personal happiness, had sought to keep aloof. Mr. Duffy, in a line of an early draft of "A Painful Case" deleted from the published story, had reiterated the artist-superman dictum: "I, he said, will receive with disdain every advance on the part of this civilization which is unworthy of me but which seeks to entrap me." [33] Joyce too, wrapped in "silence, exile and cunning," will attempt to maintain artistic inviolability in the face of public disfavor.

The main character of the play is Alfred Loth, a dangerous and volatile young man just returned from a spell in prison for his part in attempting to establish a Utopia in the United States. Punished by society for a nonconformist idealism which it can never understand, he speaks with approval of his hot-headed days at college and insists, as does Stephen-Joyce, "I'm done with sham religion and sham morals." [34] Rebel, exile, criminal, apostate, young Loth makes this pronouncement to a man named Hoffmann, his opposite in every detail. Hoffmann is rich, conservative, middle-class, living in comfortable paralysis in a city that honors his mediocrity and fears the power of his money. The Shem-Shaun relationship of the *Wake* may be delineated here in 1901 for the artist who was to publish it in 1939. In a silky voice,

Hoffmann advises his suspect visitor that "One must proceed
on feasible lines, on practicable lines," and then expresses his
belief, undoubtedly justified, that Loth would "proceed on
extremely impracticable lines." Recommending hypocrisy,
the Shaun-like prototype suggests working from above, not
with, the poor, in order to avoid the appearance of evil intent.[35] Shaun, the fair-haired boy, persecutor of his outspoken black-sheep brother, must maintain his innocent
façade, though in *Before Sunrise* he confesses to Loth's accu-
sation of swindling and, by forcing his victim to suicide, of
murder. Though the Shem-Shaun parallel is capable of
further extension, it is enough, I think, merely to suggest here
the interesting possibility.

In Alfred Loth, Joyce could have found, in addition to the
wide background of Stephen as artist, the stylistic manner of
representing his priggish young man. Brash in his loud de-
nunciation of his lost belief and his abandoned conventional
morality, Loth, like Stephen, relies on tight-lipped understatement and Wildean irony for his impact on other people
and on the audience. His habit of straight-faced, direct verbal
assault on those whom he openly acknowledges as his enemies
is a possible prelude to Stephen's daring attacks. Thus, Loth
will borrow money from Hoffmann almost in the same breath
as he accuses his rich associate of murder. Stephen, accepting
Bloom's hospitality, intrudes anti-Semitism into their conversation. Understatement, as a common technique of Joyce
and Hauptmann, is particularly effective. Loth, for instance,
refusing an alcoholic drink, draws surprised comment from
Hoffmann because "it is not the usual thing." The young
man's reply – in the tongue-in-cheek manner of *Stephen Hero*
replying to a Jesuit teacher – cuts to the bone: "I am sorry to
say you are right as to that." Like Stephen at one time during
his early career, Loth is an ascetic: "I am thoroughly satisfied
with the normal pleasures that reach my sensory system." He
has taken the pledge of total abstinence, with the rhetorical
aplomb of a religious ritual: "I am absolutely determined

to hand on to my posterity, full and undiminished, the inheritance which I have received." [36] Partly to shock, partly because he believes what he says in terms of his own character, Loth avers that he would marry, if financial conditions were favorable and if he could be sure of the physical and mental health of his marital partner. When told that he expects too much, his answer – Stephen's to a tee – is simply, "But I also make demands on myself, you must remember." [37]

It would be wrong to push these superficial evidences of similarity between the two authors any further on the basis of available proof. My final and rather detailed example of what Joyce did with the material which he read will attempt to illustrate a deliberate focus of artistic attention on the writing of one unimportant and uninspiring author – one in whose personal life there was little to admire and whose works offered to the serious artist no inspiration. Joyce's controlled borrowing in this instance is in the interest of establishing a significant motif or pattern to supplement the scores of additional motifs which pervade his longer works. In selecting the raw materials of this pattern, the young author remained true to his habits of craftsmanship: his need for analogies and correspondences, his delight in free association, and his eschewing of chronological narrative as understood in nineteenth-century fiction, in favor of elaborate motif, the insistent reiteration of a meaningful name or situation or gesture throughout one of his works.

I should like to show how one minor pattern is the result of an effective combination of the many techniques here mentioned. Though the ability of a master craftsman to combine several methods may be viewed merely as a *tour de force*, like compressing the names of six hundred rivers into the Anna Livia Plurabelle section of the *Wake*, I hope to show the vital, practical importance to Joyce's novel of the cohesiveness that merging his various but related techniques provides. Specifically, I want to point out how, by introducing the life and

D

works of Leo Taxil, mentioned only twice in *Ulysses* (U 42, 385) but inconspicuously present throughout, Joyce weaves at least eight meaningful threads into one strand to guide the reader through the fictional labyrinth. The references to Taxil involve autobiographical correspondences, [38] the theme of change in the Proteus episode, the theme of the cuckolded husband, the thread of anti-Catholic blasphemy, the theme of anti-Semitism, the Freemasonry theme, the impostor-pretender theme, and the subsidiary theme of the life of Jesus, with overtones of the book by Renan.

Though a study of *Ulysses* falls beyond the range of "The Early Fiction," I think it proper to discuss the Leo Taxil motif here as an example of how Joyce stored away memories of his youthful reading for later use. There is little doubt that his information about Taxil was acquired very early in his adult life. After 1907, the year in which Taxil died, he was quickly forgotten by all except the writers of encyclopedias. During his spectacular life, however, his escapades filled many columns of newspapers and magazines. Two full-length treatments of his career appeared in middlebrow journals in the United States in 1900. The books that he had written in the closing years of the nineteenth century were appearing in translation on the Continent during the impressionable Stephen-Joyce's stay in 1902–1903. A glance at the Dublin newspapers published around Bloomsday will show the contemporaneous interest in the coming of J. Alexander Dowie, Joyce's false prophet in *Ulysses*, and will testify to Joyce's ability to retain information acquired during his apprenticeship for later use.

The reader first sees the name of Taxil in the heart of the Proteus episode, as Stephen Dedalus meditates philosophically, alone on the beach at Sandymount:

He halted. I have passed the way to aunt Sara's. Am I not going there? Seems not. No-one about. He turned northeast and crossed the firmer sand towards the Pigeonhouse.
– *Que* [sic] *vous a mis dans cette fichue position?*

– *C'est le pigeon, Joseph.*
Patrice, home on furlough, lapped warm milk with me in the
bar MacMahon. Son of the wild goose, Kevin Egan of Paris.
My father's a bird, he lapped the sweet *lait chaud* with pink
young tongue, plump bunny's face. Lap, *lapin*. He hopes to win
in the *gros lots*. About the nature of women he read in Michelet.
But he must send me *La Vie de Jesus* by M. Leo Taxil. Lent it to
his friend. (U 42)

Walking toward the Pigeonhouse, a kind of power house
and fort built at the end of a breakwater in Dublin Bay,
Stephen lets his mind play on the associations which the name
of the imposing structure evokes. Pigeon in his mind is replaced by dove, which in turn becomes The Dove, the Holy
Ghost. Since the relation of father to son and son to father
is at the symbolic core of the book, Joyce allows Stephen's
stream of consciousness to dwell upon the part which the
Holy Ghost traditionally plays in the story of Christ's nativity.
Thus, the first paragraph quoted above is followed by an
apocryphal two-line dialogue between Joseph of Nazareth and
his wife Mary. In it Joyce is simply carrying forward the motif
of blasphemy enunciated by Buck Mulligan in the Tele-
machus episode, in the jingle which Stephen there calls "The
Ballad of Joking Jesus":

— I'm the queerest young fellow that ever you heard.
My mother's a jew, my father's a bird . . . . (U 20)

But why should the dialogue be in French, and why should
it take the precise form which it does? The fact that the Proteus episode (U 38–51) deals with change in all of its manifestations – shifting of tides, winds, sands, grammatical
usages, languages, people, and so on – is a partial but in-
sufficient explanation, for the dialogue might just as well have
been written in Sanskrit. It is true that Stephen is thinking of
Paris and that French words and expressions dot the page.
But the reason for the form of the question and the use of
French to frame it is more specific. It is to be found in Joyce's
casual reference to M. Leo Taxil, at the end of the excerpt

quoted above. Many hundreds of pages farther on in *Ulysses*, in the Oxen of the Sun episode, Joyce makes his clue more obvious when he says that "*M. Léo Taxil nous a dit que qui l'avait mise dans cette fichue position c'était le sacré pigeon, ventre de Dieu!*" (U 385) ["Mr. Leo Taxil has told us that the one who put her in this pitiful state was the holy dove, *ventre de Dieu!*"]

Joyce seems to have taken his cue for the two lines in French from the anticlerical rantings of Gabriel Jogand-Pagès, who, writing under the pseudonym of Leo Taxil, published numerous scurrilous works during the last quarter of the nineteenth century. In 1880, the Frenchman published a three-volume work of blasphemy entitled *Calotte et Calotins: Histoire du Clergé*,[39] from which Joyce appears to have taken unholy comfort. The opening of the second volume is typical of the level of argumentation which follows, "Pour avoir la foi, il faut être un imbécile; cela est certain." [40] ["To believe one must be an imbecile; that is sure."] Having established the proper mental set for his readers with this arresting start, Taxil goes on to show, anticipating Frazer's *The Golden Bough*, that the beliefs and rituals of Christianity existed in recognizable outline long before Christ entered the world. By the time Taxil reaches the section with which Joyce is concerned in *Ulysses*, he had worked himself into a mood of fierce indignation.

In a chapter entitled "Jésus, Marie, Joseph," Taxil tries to prove, from Holy writ, that the Mary–Joseph–Holy Ghost relationship was very much an eternal triangle on the strictly carnal level.

L'Évangile nous dit que Marie a enfanté tout en restant vierge. Cet accouchement virginal est passablement rigolo . . . . Marie avait fait au temple vœu de virginité, et Dieu, en la mettant enceinte de Jésus, a trouvé le truc de ne pas lui faire violer ce voeu; soit, trois fois soit.

[The Gospel tells us that Mary brought forth a child while remaining a virgin. This virginal confinement is tolerably amusing . . . . Mary had taken a vow of virginity in the temple, and God, in making her pregnant with Jesus, discovered a device to make her not break this vow; amen, three times amen.]

Taxil is now ready to spring his trap. "Mais comment Marie est-elle restée vierge lorsqu'elle a mis au monde les frères et sœurs dudit Jésus?" ["But how did Mary remain virgin when she brought into the world the brothers and sisters of said Jesus?"] He points out that Matthew records the names of four brothers of Jesus – James, Joseph, Simon and Jude, "sans comptor des sœurs." [41] ["not counting sisters."] Now he sets the scene of which Joyce's two-line dialogue is the imaginary denouement:

Joseph, disent-ils – ce n'est pas moi qui ai inventé le mot, c'est eux, – Joseph n'est pour Jésus qu'un père putatif. . . .
Sans compter que Joseph joue de son côté un rôle diablement ridicule. Voyez-vous ce pauvre bonhomme de charpentier à qui Dieu fait épouser une jeune brune, tout en lui ordonnant de s'abstenir. Puis, arrive un ange Gabriel, qui, profitant d'un moment où il n'y était pas, entre chez lui par la fenêtre et tourne à Marie . . . .
Je ne vois pas trop pourquoi Joseph n'eut pas un peu d'humeur, lorsqu'il vit sa femme grosse sans qu'il s'en fût mêlé; car enfin Gabriel ne daigna pas lui apparaître, à lui. Il est très louable d'avoir confiance en sa femme; mais il faut avoir une foi bien robuste pour croire, sur sa simple affirmation, que le bon Dieu vient lui faire des enfants par le ministère d'un ange. [42]

[Joseph, they say – I didn't invent the word, they did – Joseph is only a putative father for Jesus . . . .
Not even taking into account that Joseph plays a deucedly silly part in his own right. Do you see this poor fellow of a carpenter to whom God has given for a wife a young brunette, commanding him at the same time to remain continent. Then comes the angel Gabriel, who, taking advantage of a minute when he was not there, enters his home through the window and turns to Mary . . . .
I don't see too clearly why Joseph was not a bit peevish when he saw his wife swell up without his being involved in it;

for after all Gabriel did not vouchsafe to appear to him. It is very praiseworthy to trust one's wife; but one must have terribly strong faith to believe, on her mere statement, that the good God comes to produce children for one through the offices of an angel.]

It is but a step from this point to Joseph's anxious question concerning the agency by which Mary was made pregnant; and to Mary's answer, "C'est le pigeon, Joseph."

In *La Vie de Jésus* (1884), which Joyce cites in *Ulysses*, Taxil repeats much of what he has said in earlier books and, going further, causes Joseph to ask the question specifically. Assuring his readers that Joseph, though good natured, was not completely naïve, he records another imaginary conversation between Mary (whom he calls "Marion") and the venerable carpenter.

– Joseph, mon gros lapin, je vous donne ma parole d'honneur que je suis toujours digne de vous . . . Aucun homme ne peut se vanter d'avoir seulement baisé le bout de mes doigts . . .
– Ta, ta, ta, je ne prends pas des vessies pour des lanternes . . . Qui donc, si ce n'est un homme, vous a mis dans cette fichue position?
– C'est le pigeon, Joseph! [43]

[Joseph, my big fellow, I give you my word of honour that I am always worthy of you . . . No man can boast of having kissed even the tips of my fingers . . .
– Ta, ta, ta, I don't make mountains out of molehills . . . Who then, if it is not a man, has put you in such a sorry state?
– It is the pigeon, Joseph!]

Quite apart from and beyond young Joyce's personal feelings about the church and his oft demonstrated enjoyment in twitting its most sacred practices in his fiction, the Mary–Joseph–Holy Ghost triangle served the writer as one more manifestation of the theme of the cuckolded husband. Universal and pervasive, the motif furnished Joyce with a favorite and frequently iterated tableau of human nature. In the *Wake*, he expresses it most dramatically in terms of the

Tristan–Iseult–Mark of Cornwall affair, as well as in the more shadowy love story of Diarmuid and Grania pursued by the giant Finn MacCool. In *Ulysses*, numerous variations on the theme blend to swell a strident chorus: Ulysses, Penelope, and the suitors; Bloom, Molly, and Blazes Boylan; Mozart's "Don Giovanni" [44] motif; with minor modifications, Bloom, Molly, and Martha Clifford; and, seldom mentioned, the sacrilegious juxtaposition of the story of the Holy Family with the household of Number 7 Eccles Street.

It is not necessary to outline the similarities in detail. That Bloom plays "un role diablement ridicule" in his own home, as Taxil says of Joseph, is patent. And though it is hard to see Blazes Boylan in the role of an angel, his safe arrival at Molly's home, "profitant d'un moment où il [Bloom] n'y était pas," links him with Taxil's perverse archangel Gabriel, at least in intent. It will be worth while, however, to examine the wholly unambiguous way in which Joyce shows that the motif was inspired by Taxil's blasphemies in almost all of its appearances in *Ulysses*.

In the Cyclops episode (U 287–339), after ironic reference to Bloom as "the new Messiah for Ireland" (U 331), the tipsy gossips in Barney Kiernan's pub discuss the Jews:

– Well, they're still waiting for their redeemer, says Martin. For that matter so are we.

– Yes, says J.J., and every male that's born they think it may be their Messiah . . . .

– Expecting every moment will be his next, says Lenehan.

– O, by God, says Ned, you should have seen Bloom before that son of his that died was born. I met him one day in the south city markets buying a tin of Neave's food six weeks before the wife was delivered.

– *En ventre sa mère*, says J.J.

– Do you call that a man? says the citizen.

– I wonder did he ever put it out of sight, says Joe.

– Well, there were two children born anyhow, says Jack Power.

– And who does he suspect? says the citizen. (U 331–332)

When the talk turns from mention of the Jews awaiting the birth of a Messiah to Bloom waiting for the birth of Rudy, the experienced reader of Joyce's novels, with Taxil's text before him, realizes the author's hint. Bloom becomes the modern-day Joseph, and Rudy, long since dead, takes on for the moment the lineaments of Christ. Confirmation of such an hypothesis appears almost immediately when the irreverent gossips and detractors – all Irish Leo Taxils – raise the question of paternity. As in Taxil's version, "Joseph n'est pour Jésus qu'un père putatif," so Bloom, to the men in the bar, is incapable of fatherhood and must suspect his cuckolded situation. Even Taxil's question, "Mais comment Marie est-elle restée vierge lorsqu'elle a mis au monde les frères et sœurs dudit Jésus?" is distortedly echoed in Jack Power's remark that Bloom's wife had more than one child. The ever present sign of Taxil's direct influence on the theme in *Ulysses* is the reiteration in French of a part of Taxil's blasphemous diatribe. Putting "*En ventre sa mère,*" in the mouth of the ignorant J.J., where it obviously does not belong, is as artificial a method of pointing to the source as the numberless combinations of word clusters with initial letters "H.C.E." to announce the presence of Earwicker in *Finnegans Wake*. This trade-mark of Taxil's influence, as I shall illustrate specifically later in this chapter, accompanies the motif, no matter what the particular context of its appearance.

That Joyce leans to the cynical explanation of Rudy's birth seems clear. Just as by implication he superimposes Molly's animality and Bloom's confirmed suspicions against the heroic backdrop of Odysseus's trust and Penelope's fidelity, so he uses the Taxil version to tarnish the Biblical account, venerable but, to him, no longer credible or comforting. If the protagonist of *Stephen Hero* could call the Holy Ghost "a spermatozoon with wings added" (S 141), Joyce was ready, at that age, for the anticlerical shafts of the French charlatan. Stephen's conversation with his mother on the Ascension of Christ might have come straight from Taxil's formidable library of illustrated blasphemies

> – Where did he [Christ] go off?
> – From Mount Olivet, answered his mother reddening under her eyes.
> – Head first?
> – What do you mean, Stephen?
> – I mean he must have been rather giddy by the time he arrived. Why didn't he go by balloon? (S 132–133) [45]

After more of the same, Stephen tells his mother that he cannot believe in these miracles. "It's absurd: it's Barnum. He comes into the world God knows how, walks on the water, gets out of his grave and goes up off the Hill of Howth. What drivel is this?" Excited and moved, as Taxil was, by Renan's works, Stephen wonders "which was better . . . Renan's account of the death of Jesus or the account given by the evangelists." (S 133, 189) [46]

In the Oxen of the Sun episode (U 377–421), Joyce again brings Taxil's theme of the cuckold to bear upon the narrative of *Ulysses*. An appropriate place for a reprise, this chapter concerns the birth of a child to Mrs. Purefoy. At the maternity hospital are "sir Leopold [Bloom] that had of his body no manchild for an heir," and Stephen Dedalus, who says, "Now drink we . . . of this mazer and quaff ye this mead which is not indeed parcel of my body but my soul's bodiment." Stephen speaks of Mary as the "second Eve":

> But here is the matter now. Or she knew him, that second I say, and was but creature of her creature . . . . or she knew him not and then stands she in the one denial or ignorancy with Peter Piscator who lives in the house that Jack built and with Joseph the Joiner patron of the happy demise of all unhappy marriages *parce que M. Léo Taxil nous a dit que qui l'avait mise dans cette fichue position c'était le sacré pigeon, ventre de Dieu!* (U 385)

Once again the insinuations and once again the French tag line announcing the presence of the Taxil point of view.

Finally, in the Circe episode (U 422–593), the theme is

suggested of Mary's carnal relationship with the Holy Ghost, as Kitty, one of the whores, speaks:

And Mary Shortall that was in the lock with the pox she got from Jimmy Pidgeon in the blue caps had a child off him that couldn't swallow and was smothered with the convulsions in the mattress and we all subscribed for the funeral. (U 509)

Taxil's line, to offer corroboration, follows immediately, this time placed in the mouth of Philip Drunk – *"Qui vous a mis dans cette fichue position, Philippe?"* To this, Philip Sober replies, *"C'était le sacré pigeon, Philippe"* (U 509). Consistent throughout, Joyce seeks to draw attention to his literary sources by labeling his borrowings. [47]

Granted that Joyce was a voracious borrower of other people's writing, why should he have chosen Leo Taxil as his source of anti-Catholic blasphemy rather than any one of a score of irreligious writers whose works were available to him? The answer seems to lie in a great many considerations, chief among which was the story of Taxil's astounding career. So notorious were his machinations to become by the beginning of the twentieth century (the time of the events in *Ulysses*) that his biography seeped down even to the matter-of-fact readers of America's *Popular Science Monthly* and *Lippincott's Magazine*. [48] Taxil himself, moreover, had written his own portrait of the quick-change artist as a young man and published it in 1886 under the title, *Confessions d'un Ex-Libre-Penseur*. [49]

Piecing the Frenchman's story together from all these accounts, Joyce would have found familiar the narrative of a pious Catholic childhood. He would have recognized the resemblance to his own training in the story of Taxil's education under the Jesuits – the little boy's fear of the "Surveillant général." (When "il paraissait à la porte d'une étude, personne n'osait plus souffler . . .") [When "he appeared at the door of a study hall, nobody dared to breathe."] Taxil's adventures in a Jesuit high school would have recalled Joyce's days at Belvedere, and the French boy's final, awful realization that he had lost the faith ("Je ne crois plus," ["I no longer believe"] Gabriel tells his teacher-priest) would have proved to the Irish author that here was a kindred spirit.[50]

Leaving the Jesuit school, Taxil began to contribute pieces to newspapers, as Joyce did in 1902–1903. In journalism he "speedily won distinction by reckless contempt for religion." Excess followed excess until, to escape imprisonment for slander and obscenity contained in an almost totally fictional, blasphemous attack on Pope Pius IX, he had to flee to Geneva where he wrote in exile for three years. Though Joyce's situation was not precisely comparable, Taxil's flight from his country to Switzerland, induced by his desire to write as he pleased, may very well have caused the Irishman to file the Taxil case in his prodigious memory for future use. That Taxil returned to Paris from exile in Switzerland, where he continued to write and to be troubled by lawsuits directed at his alleged blasphemous and obscene writings made the analogy even more fitting. The appropriate climax to this stage of the Frenchman's career came when, as Gabriel Jogand-Pagès, he changed his name to Leo Taxil, at his father's request, to avoid dishonoring the respectable name of his provincial family. Though an early version of the opening page of Joyce's *Portrait* identifies the mother as Mrs. Joyce and the tiny "artist" as "Jim" (James Joyce), it is interesting to note that in the final account, for whatever reason, the family name has become "Dedalus."[51]

With Taxil's return to Paris and his proprietorship of an anticlerical bookstore, most of the manifest analogies between his life and that of Joyce end. Taxil continued to write books attacking the practices and the men of the Church; and to fan the fires daily, he published a newspaper called *L'Anti-Clérical*. From this point on, while the story of his life impinges meaningfully on the fictional life of Leopold Bloom and Stephen Dedalus in *Ulysses*, autobiographical similarities cease. But the fact that Joyce has Stephen speak of Taxil implies that he was conscious of the likeness. If he was impressed by coincidental patterns of autobiographical detail in the life of Swift, one may speculate with good reason on the importance to him of the contemporary analogical pattern displayed by his French counterpart.

What happens to Taxil in 1885 explains, I think, his presence in the Proteus episode. Taxil himself writes of the shock of his own reconversion to Catholicism, which occurs as he sits at his desk writing a derogatory history of Joan of Arc:

> Tout à coup, j'éprouvai comme une secousse formidable dans tout mon être. Il me sembla qu'une voix intérieure me criait:
> – Fou que tu es! halluciné toi-même! tu ne comprends donc pas que Jeanne est une sainte.

> [Suddenly, I felt, as it were, a tremendous shock through my whole being. It seemed to me that an inner voice cried out to me:
> – What a fool you are! you are the deluded one! you do not understand, therefore, that Joan is a saint.]

Taxil then sees clearly his recent sinful past and contrasts it with the joys and innocence of his childhood, the age of belief –

> Et j'éclatai en sanglots.
> – Pardon, mon Dieu! . . . pardon pour mes blasphèmes! pardon pour tout le mal dont je me suis rendu coupable! [52]

> [And I burst into tears.
> – Forgiveness, oh God! . . . pardon for my sins! pardon for all the wickedness of which I am guilty!]

Though there were many who rightly doubted the sincerity of his conversion, he entered upon the next phase with the zeal of a soul snatched back from Hell. He closed his shop, suppressed his own blasphemies, asked for and, at the hands of the papal nuncio, received absolution from the sentence of excommunication that had earlier been passed upon him.

But these were negative acts. Taxil's flair for the dramatic led him to demonstrate vividly his break with the past and his leadership in the Faith Militant. He had earlier (in 1881) joined the Freemasons as an apprentice, the lowest rank, and had had almost no experience with the order. Now, in 1886, he began a series of alleged exposures of the Freemasons as anti-Catholic and, in fact, anti-Christ. He filled his long tracts, often running to three volumes, with the brashest lies about the practices and principles of an organization he knew almost nothing about. Without bothering to offer proof (which he did not and could not have), he accused the order of the grossest obscenities and the most terrifying objectives.

The deception proved highly profitable. His books on Freemasonry sold in unbelievable numbers and his presence as a lecturer, at lucrative fees, was in great demand. Moreover, he was hailed for his work by the highest rank of the Church hierarchy. Pope Leo XIII received him in audience in 1887, praised his books, and told him, "Thy life is still very useful in combats for the faith." The whole-hearted acceptance of his baseless charges against the Freemasons led Taxil next to his most ambitious deception – "one of the crassest and most impudent and yet most successful frauds of modern times . . . ." The "Diana Vaughan" hoax need not be dwelt on at length here, for Joyce appears not to have been concerned with it. Yet Joyce must have relished Taxil's ability to palm off upon the unsuspecting clergy – from country curate to Pope Leo – an American stenographer living in Paris and employed by him, as the spouse of the devil Asmodeus and the daughter of the goddess Astarte. The idea of Taxil exorcising the devils which sought to break down her will to resist their evil advances would have amused him, but the reception in clerical circles of the Catholic prayer book prepared by Taxil and published under the name of Diana Vaughan would have struck him as ludicrously incongruous. Even gross Shaun's hypocritical commencement address to the schoolgirls in *Finnegans Wake* is less startling. A cardinal wrote to Diana thanking his "dear daughter" for the pages which she had sent him and saying that he was reading them "with burning interest." In return he sent the "special benediction of his Holiness." Even the secretary to Pope Leo XIII thanked her and asked that she "continue to write and to unmask the godless sect."

Knowing that the bubble must eventually burst – and half wishing for the notoriety of exposure, which would discredit the gullible clergy – Taxil received the plaudits of a large portion both of lay and clerical adherents. With wry modesty and an ironic hint of things to come, he announced slyly, "One can never be sure of a converted Freemason but must always fear lest he may return to his former friends. Not until the convert is dead can one be wholly free from this anxiety. I am well aware that this general principle applies also to myself." His charming personal reservations, however, merely strengthened those who believed completely in the truth of his role. The end came when the demand of the faithful and the cynical that Diana Vaughan be produced could no longer be stilled. On April 19, 1897, seven years in advance of Bloomsday, standing before a large French audience in a public hall, Taxil revealed the deception: "Reverend sirs, ladies and gentlemen! You wish to see Diana Vaughan. Look at me! I myself am that lady!" After he had explained the details of his scheme, it was easy to see why he had had the audience check its weapons at the door. The infuriated crowd pursued its tormentor unsuccessfully through the streets. But during the period of the hoax, Taxil had made half a million francs from donations sent by the credulous to Diana Vaughan.

Trickster, practical joker, baiter of gullible prelates, Taxil bore a strong resemblance to Joyce's self-portrait of the artist as a young man. Oliver Gogarty has recently defined "Artist" in Joyce's title as "practical joker"; and how many critics were to say of Joyce later what an enemy of Taxil is reported to have said of the slippery Frenchman: "Taxil knew better than many well-instructed Catholics the facts and the teaching of the Church in the difficult and abstruse matter of supernatural manifestations, and he had succeeded in his fraudulent work only by resting it on this solid foundation."[53] Turning the teachings of their excellent Jesuit preceptors against their mentors, both Joyce and Taxil had scandalized respectable citizens. Taxil retains a place in *The Catholic Encyclopedia* only under the heading of "Impostors," where he is credited with having "brought home to our own generation" the "dangers of excessive credulity" through his "outrageous impostures."[54]

The Proteus episode is the chapter of change and imposture. The goddess Eidothee in Homer describes the shifting and changing of Proteus, the Old Man of the Sea:

> Directly you see him settled, summon all your strength and courage and hold him down however hard he strains and struggles to escape. He will try all kinds of transformations, and change himself not only into every sort of beast on earth, but into water too and blazing fire. But hold him fast and grip him all the tighter.[55]

Menelaus, in the *Odyssey*, tells how Proteus is finally cornered:

> . . . we leapt upon him and flung our arms round his back. But the old man's skill and cunning had not deserted him. He began by turning into a bearded lion and then into a snake, and after that a panther and a giant boar. He changed into running water too and a great tree in leaf. But we set our teeth and held him like a vice.[56]

So too in Joyce's Proteus episode everything changes – tides move, the sun is obscured by clouds, sands shift, thoughts fleet by, language undergoes basic changes (i.e., "I am almosting it") (U 47), and history is described as a shifting panorama. In such a setting, Taxil's career seems almost an artistically contrived pattern of change to fit the needs of the motif and the plot. First a pious Catholic, then an impious unbeliever, then a militant son of the Church obtrusively though hypocritically fighting for the faith, finally a

self-induced outcast officially listed as an impostor, Taxil
represents, in his relationship to Catholicism, an ideal symbol
to reinforce the central theme of the episode.

The motif of imposture is almost as strong in Proteus as
that of change. Buck Mulligan has already been branded a
"Usurper" (U 24) for demanding Stephen's key to the tower.
Then, in the Proteus episode, Stephen calls the roll of
impostors and pretenders:

> A primrose doublet, fortune's knaves [Haines and Mulligan]
> smiled on my fear. For that are you pining, the bark of their
> applause? Pretenders: live their lives. The Bruce's brother,
> Thomas Fitzgerald, silken knight, Perkin Warbeck, York's
> false scion, in breeches of silk of whiterose ivory, wonder of a
> day, and Lambert Simnel . . . . Paradise of pretenders then and
> now . . . . (U 46)

Joyce's penchant for layer upon layer of elaboration in the
working out of a motif is too well known to require restate-
ment here. The inclusion of Taxil in the episode is plainly
meant to link the most notorious of contemporary religious
pretenders to the imposture motif of Proteus and *Ulysses*.
Stephen admonishes himself to "live their lives," and, in a
sense, Joyce is living Taxil's life.

In his use of Taxil's name early in the century, Joyce could
have counted on a wide area of recognition. The Frenchman
was still alive and writing in 1904, at the time of Bloomsday,
and his writings were available in English, German, Italian,
and Spanish translations. When he died in 1907, the story of
his lurid career was widely recalled for its human interest.
Writing the Proteus episode not long after the appearance of
these obituaries, Joyce could have expected the same degree
of recognition for Taxil as a contemporary reader might grant
Billy Sunday.

Beyond the strengthening of the central patterns of Proteus,
Joyce may have had in mind when he chose Taxil the enrich-
ment of the theme of anti-Semitism in *Ulysses*. After his conversion in 1885, as has been said, Taxil busied himself in two

main pursuits: proving the ostensible genuineness of his Catholicism and fighting all enemies of the Faith. Such activities soon brought him into conflict with the French journalist and politician Edouard Drumont, one of the most outspoken French anti-Semites of the 1890s.[57] Though the origins of the dispute between the two men are obscure, the feud burst into the open when Taxil opposed Drumont's election to office. The convert even sought to give testimony in court of a conspiracy, purportedly involving Drumont, to massacre all Jews. As Drumont explains it in *Le Testament d'un antisémite* (1891), his side sought to show that Taxil's testimony could not be reliable since the witness had written such books as the blasphemous *La Vie de Jésus*, in which "l'ignoble est partout."[58] ["the ignoble is everywhere."]

The best way for Drumont to discredit Taxil was to show that his words were colored by pro-Semitic leanings. Still speaking of Taxil's blasphemies, therefore, Drumont adds:

> La Vierge est couverte d'immodices. Tout ce qui la concerne est, d'ailleurs, le développement d'un calomnie abjecte du Talmaud que j'ai déjà flétrie et qui nous montre la Vierge accoupleuse de femmes et engrossée par un soldat nommé Panther . . . .

> [The Virgin is covered with filth. Everything that concerns her, besides, is the unfolding of a low Talmudic slander which I have already demolished and which shows us the Virgin paired with women and made pregnant by a soldier called Panther . . . .]

Jeered by the spectators in the courtroom when he tried to testify about the projected massacre of the Hebrews, Taxil was interrupted by the judge, who asked him if he was the author of *La Vierge aux latrines*. The authorship acknowledged, Taxil was castigated by the judge as unfit to appear in public. Amid deafening applause, he was told to hide himself from honest citizens.

> La vérité est que s'il avait roulé les poires catholiques, avec sa "conversion" il avait également roulé les poires israélites en se

E

faisant subventionner par elles et en les assurant qu'il allait ne faire qu'une bouchée de Drumont . . . .[59]

[The truth is that if he had cheated the Catholic "suckers" with his "conversion," he had cheated the Jewish "suckers" alike in having himself subsidized by them and in assuring them that he was going to make a mere mouthful out of Drumont . . . .]

Not one to remain silent in a battle of polemics, Taxil produced a full-length book on *Monsieur Drumont: Étude psychologique* (1890), in which he promises to expose the real Drumont as not only anti-Semitic but anti-Catholic. He had learned the value of sweeping generalities and extravagant claims through the success of his antimasonic tracts. Hence his suspenseful opening: "Je sais qu'en province un assez grand nombre de conservateurs qui avaient la naïveté de croire au catholicisme de M. Drumont, vont être stupéfaits en apprenant ces choses."[60] ["I know that in the country quite a large number of conservatives who were naïve enough to believe in Mr. Drumont's Catholicism are going to be amazed to learn these things."] But first Taxil must present his own credentials. He defies anyone to find a single act or line or word of his, since his converson in 1885, which is not above reproach. Moreover, he is not a Jew. He is a Catholic by birth and by conversion:

> Et ce n'est pas cette seconde manière qui est la moins appréciable; car le fait d'embrasser la religion, quand on a l'âge d'homme, quand on est dans tout son bon sens, dans la pleine expérience de la vie, le fait de se vouer à défendre le catholicisme attaqué de toutes parts, ce fait-là est certainement très caractéristique.
>
> Par le cœur aussi bien que par les origines, je descends donc en droite ligne, non de Sem, mais de Japhet. Je suis de race aryenne, sans qu'un seul descendant d'Abraham soit venu mêler son sang à celui de mes ancêtres.[61]

[And this second way is not the least considerable; for the act of embracing religion, when one reaches man's estate, when one is of sound mind, in the full experience of life, the act of promising to defend Catholicism attacked on all sides, such an act is surely very revelatory of strong character. In my heart as well as through ancestry, I descend, therefore, in a straight line, not from Shem, but from Japhet. I am of Aryan stock, without a single descendant of Abraham having mixed his blood with that of my ancestors.]

In Taxil's indictment of Drumont for his "jew obsession" the motif of anti-Semitism in *Ulysses* receives reinforcement. What is said of Drumont here might very appropriately have been applied to The Citizen, as he appears in the Cyclops episode, and to a strong vein of anti-Semitic sentiment in Ireland at the time of Bloomsday. Complaining of Drumont's unreasoning concern with Jews, Taxil adds, "Il voit des juifs partout, en tout le mal qui arrive provient des juifs." He goes on, "Le juif est son cauchemar. Il le découvre dans toutes les œuvres de la politique, et même dans les moindres incidents de la vie privée."[62] ["He sees Jews everywhere, in all the bad that happens Jews are involved. . . . The Jew is his nightmare. He finds him in every political activity, and even in the smallest occurrences of private life."] Taxil proposes a series of rhetorical questions and answers which he attributes to men of Drumont's mentality:

Qui a fondé la franc-maçonnerie? qui la dirige?
Ce sont les juifs.
Qui est cause de malaise général des affaires?
Ce sont les juifs.

[Who established Freemasonry? who runs it?
The Jews.
Who is responsible for the general unrest of business?
The Jews.]

In short, in Taxil's pungent words, Drumont has discovered "l'odeur de juif." Either operating on his own or borrowing the colorful image, Joyce lets the narrator of the Cyclops episode elaborate on the same expression: "So they started talking about capital punishment and of course Bloom comes

out with the why and the wherefor and all the codology of the
business and the old dog smelling him all the time I'm told
those Jewies does have a sort of a queer odour coming off
them for dogs . . ." (U 299).

There is no question either that Joyce had discovered
"l'odeur de Drumont," and little question that he was
familiar with the Taxil-Drumont controversy. For, buried in
the Proteus episode, where Taxil makes his original appearance, is a reference to "M. Drumont, famous journalist"
(U 44), that for many years mystified me by its apparently
random appearance little more than a page beyond the
Taxil quotation. In an episode that beautifully illustrates the
artistic effectiveness of free association as a controlled literary
technique, the mental leap from Taxil to Drumont seems a
natural progression once the reader has the necessary his-
torical background to comprehend the connection between
the two men. That this connection should hinge on the relationship of both figures to Catholicism and to the Jewish
Question is eminently fitting in a book whose hero is Leopold
Bloom – Jew by ancestry, nonpracticing Catholic by marriage,
scapegoat by circumstance.

The sort of question which Taxil attributes to Drumont
("Qui est cause du malaise general des affaires?") and its
hypothetical answer ("Ce sont les juifs") are constantly put
and occasionally responded to in *Ulysses*. Mr. Deasy, in the
Nestor episode (U 25–37), insists that

> . . . England is in the hands of the jews. In all the highest
> places: her finance, her press. And they are the signs of a
> nation's decay. Wherever they gather they eat up the nation's
> vital strength. I have seen it coming these years. As sure as we
> are standing here the jew merchants are already at their work
> of destruction. Old England is dying. (U 34)

Ignorant Michael Cusack, The Citizen, with his talk of
"swindling the peasants . . . and the poor of Ireland," and
his insistence that "we want no more strangers in our house"
(U 318), carries on in the Drumont tradition. And Bloom,

peaceful to a fault, reserved and self-effacing, feels it necessary to take a position with regard to organized anti-Semitism: "... I belong to a race too ... that is hated and persecuted. Also now. This very moment. This very instant" (U 326).

To multiply examples of the prevalence of the theme in *Ulysses* for readers of that novel is unnecessary and for others futile. Bloom's answer to general accusations against his race is the key to the last facet of the Leo Taxil motif which I wish to treat. "Force, hatred, history, all that. That's not life for men and women, insult and hatred. And everybody knows that it's the very opposite of that that is really life." When asked what he means, he answers, "Love ... I mean the opposite of hatred" (U 327). As Mr. Leonard Albert has shown, such statements roughly approximate the general Masonic doctrine of universal brotherhood and love.[63] Albert develops the thesis that Joyce was much interested in Freemasonry, that many obscure passages in *Ulysses* are explicable in terms of Masonic ritual or doctrine, and that Leopold Bloom proves that he is a Mason in his own right by finger signs; by his charitable feelings; by being the recipient of the entreaty, "Charitable mason, pray for us" (U 488); and by his actual invoking of the Masonic oath (U 283) at the moment when Stephen Dedalus reminds him of his dead son Rudy. As Albert sees it, "the theme of Freemasonry ... is *Joyce's* [*sic*] symbol of fraternal, and paternal love."[64]

Taxil's writings on Freemasonry are voluminous and complicated. This is not the place to attempt a thorough treatment of them, or even of Joyce's possible borrowing from them. The important point here is that by using Taxil's name in *Ulysses*, Joyce is able unobtrusively – maybe too unobtrusively – to elaborate upon, to justify, and to give depth to his scattered references to the Masons. At the same time he is able to endow the apparently aimless references with a point of view, a focus, without resorting to the didacticism and explicit moralizing of writers like George Eliot or Hardy or

Butler. For the reader who knows of the Taxil-Freemasonry fiasco, the "exposure" of the Masons by Joyce in his novel acquires an additional dimension. We know how to take his straight-faced revelations. By juxtaposing the role of Taxil and the role of Joyce, the author of *Ulysses* is able to play up the comic aspects of his novel with an absolute economy in the use of words.

The disadvantage, on the other hand, of such obscure labyrinthine motifs as Joyce delights in introducing is considerable. The materials of free association must be those which would naturally find a place in the fleeting thoughts of the characters of the novel – local allusions, contemporary music-hall songs, headlines from yesterday's newspapers. That such ephemeral evidences of everyday living will mean the same thing – or anything – to the reader who attempts to follow the associational thread half a century later is doubtful. Nor can all of the references to the specific events and environment of Bloomsday, June 16, 1904, be given universal, timeless overtones by the author if he wishes, at the same time, to preserve the integrity of the characters as realistic living people with a normal flow of consciousness.

Joyce was probably right to concentrate his attention on re-creating this normal flow without regard to the difficulties which future generations of readers might face. The popularity of *Ulysses* among those who give the book a chance to register its impact is a crude but meaningful way to judge its effectiveness after thirty-five years before the reading public. For every motif whose original force has been blunted by the shifting focus of history, another motif hits home sharply and without ambiguity. A stray word can send the reader's mind along a new track, allowing much to be implied by the author when little is explained. In this kind of writing a network of associations and motifs replaces traditional chronology of the nineteenth-century narrative. Some patterns – the Leo Taxil reference, for instance – are less successful with the contemporary reader in carrying the weight of meaning that Joyce assigned them to bear for the "ideal reader" whom he envisaged. These patterns, now, are the province of the scholars. Joyce's reading often provides the key.

Dubliners is the most immediately Irish of Joyce's works. Its scenes, usually uncomplicated by elaborate analogical elements – Homeric or other mythic diversions – are less universal in reference than those of *Ulysses*, with its pervasive mythic undercurrents, or of the *Wake*, with its centripetal word melodies. The private, autobiographical touch is strong and lyrical. That this should be so is natural, for the stories, many of them certainly, were written or planned while the author still lived on the scene and was involved as a human being. In addition to his discovery, communicated later to Arthur Power,[1] that all writers must be first representative of their national tradition, his recorded purpose in writing the stories at all precluded any attempt to internationalize or overcivilize his dour observations. For if *Dubliners* is Joyce's attempt, as he puts it, to give the "Irish people . . . one good look at themselves in my nicely polished looking-glass,"[2] it had to contain as honest and straightforward a presentation of the national environment as an artist could achieve. What is more, Joyce had before him as he planned his stories the sensible advice that William Archer had given him earlier to restrict his range deliberately, to use a few well-developed characters in each piece, and especially to avoid diffuse and complicated symbolic structures, "hieroglyphics" meaningless even to such sensitive and erudite readers as Ibsen's translator.[3]

That Joyce goes too far in the direction of drab, matter-of-fact plot material, couched in a "style of scrupulous meanness," is clear to those who have examined the first published version of "The Sisters" as it appeared in *The Irish Homestead*.[4] Though I have dealt elsewhere with symbolic elements of this early story, in terms of their alteration from one draft to another, and although Hugh Kenner has made observations on Joyce's changing intent,[5] I feel that there is much value to be derived from further careful analysis of the changes that occur. The existence of still a third draft,[6] in manuscript, showing the progress of the story between the *Homestead* and the final *Dubliners* version, makes consideration imperative for students of Joyce's early prose.

The *Homestead* draft reveals the young author apparently trying to follow Archer's strictures to the letter, and trying as well as to satisfy the editor of the magazine, who had requested something "simple" and "rural," something likely to please "the common understanding & liking." "The Sisters," in that early stage, is little more than an extended epiphany and requires just about half as many words as the final version to tell the story. The *Homestead* draft is an adequate character sketch of a dead priest as he appeared to a small boy and others who had known him in his later years. Though it is presented from the point of view of the boy, the telling does not reveal the boy to us except in the most mechanical and pedestrian way. Nor does it really illuminate the actual relationship between the young narrator and his elderly acquaintance. For all the reader knows about that relationship when he finishes reading the early draft, the boy might have been almost a paid companion who came occasionally to sit with the old invalid and to humor him by responding impersonally to the patient's whims. In other words, there is no real relationship established in the *Homestead* version; the story might have been narrated just as effectively by the aunt of the boy or by Cotter or even by one of the sisters. There are no universal implications nor is there any room for symbolism. The only important character is dead when the story opens. This one-leveled and not very imaginative sketch offers little encouragement to those who would insist that Joyce never made a mistake in literary creation.

Even while he was writing the story for the *Homestead*, the young writer must have realized that it was artistically weak. Perhaps Archer's advice had inhibited him and temporarily stifled his flair for meaningful elaboration. Maybe George Russell's insistence on predigested fiction had affected his judgment. It is possible too that Joyce was simply not ready to produce first-rate stories early in 1904 – hardly a likely alternative since many of his finest attempts were to be made during the next twelve months. If Joyce could praise Ibsen because the playwright's work contains "from first to last" scarcely "a superfluous word or phrase," then the Irishman must have been dissatisfied with his own story, for, in the process of revision,[7] he doubled the number of words and phrases which the original draft contained. The student must assume that the author, as he progressed in skill and experience and perhaps confidence, found these additions absolutely essential.

The need for unity and coherence in the volume of fifteen short stories may account for certain additions to the story, conceived and published separately. Looked at this way, perhaps the oriental motif which finds its way into the final version is not needed in the slighter sketch, where it does not operate to strengthen analogous motifs in "Araby" and "A Little Cloud."

The additions to the bare narrative outlines of the *Homestead* version are these: the motif of paralysis; the dreams and reveries of the boy, which show his relationship with the dead priest in a new dimension; the oriental motif already mentioned; simony and confession; and the imaginative symbolic framework, admissible on no other grounds, of the boy's relationship to his religion, as suggested by his reaction to wine and wafer, to the death of Father Flynn, and to prayer.

The inclusion of paralysis as Father Flynn's affliction in the *Dubliners* version of "The Sisters" may be ascribed simply to literary expediency. The volume of short stories is to be, in Joyce's well-known words, "a chapter of the moral history of my country and I chose Dublin for the scene because that city seemed to me the centre of paralysis." [8] It would follow that, by introducing a paralyzed human being on the first page of the book – a person, moreover, representative of the most influential group in Ireland at the time – the author would be directing the attention of his readers to the major motif immediately, and as dramatically as possible. In the *Homestead* story, the ambiguity surrounding the death of the priest is never resolved. The reader is not given sufficient background to let him develop an attitude toward the key action of the narrative. In the final draft Joyce goes further than usual toward explicit statement, in order to establish his reference to paralysis as particularly important, telling the reader that the word "had always sounded strangely in my ears, like . . . the word simony in the Catechism. But now it sounded to me like the name of some maleficent and sinful being. It filled me with fear, and yet I longed to be nearer to it and to look upon its deadly work" (D 7).

The mention of simony, here merely an ugly illustrative simile, becomes vaguely sinister as Joyce repeats it in another context a bit farther on in the story. In a long paragraph, omitted entirely from both earlier drafts, Joyce introduces several puzzling references:

> It was late when I fell asleep. Though I was angry with old Cotter for alluding to me as a child, I puzzled my head to extract meaning from his unfinished sentences. In the dark of my room I imagined that I saw again the heavy grey face of the paralytic. I drew the blankets over my head and tried to think of Christmas. But the grey face still followed me. It murmured; and I understood that it desired to confess something. I felt my soul receding into some pleasant and vicious region; and there again I found it waiting for me. It began to confess to me in a murmuring voice and I wondered why it smiled continually and why the lips were so moist with spittle. But then I remembered that it had died of paralysis and I felt that I too was smiling feebly as if to absolve the simoniac of his sin. (D 9-10)

Elsewhere I have suggested that "The Sisters" deals indirectly with Joyce's own painful time of indecision about his possible vocation for the priesthood. In such a context, the paragraph is more meaningful. The dead priest, in the final version of the story, becomes the representative of a paralyzed religion whose mysteries both attract and repel the child. Like the priest in *A Portrait* who, his face in darkness, loops a noose as he holds out prospects of a life in the Jesuit order for Stephen Dedalus, Father Flynn is reported – only in the *Dubliners* version – to have "had a great wish for him" (D 8). On what other basis can he consider himself a "simoniac" but in his holding out of ecclesiastical preferment to his young charge? Joyce even suggests that payment is made by the boy for such favors. Significantly, the author alters a seemingly inconsequential detail of the *Homestead* draft so that it will fit in with the motif of simony. The early story says:

> My aunt, who is what they call good-hearted, never went into the shop without bringing him some High Toast, and he used to take the packet of snuff from her hands, gravely inclining his head for sign of thanks.

In the revised version in *Dubliners*, this has become:

> Perhaps my aunt would have given *me* a packet of High Toast for him and this present would have roused him from his stupefied doze. It was always *I* who emptied the packet into his black snuff-box . . . . (D 11) [*Italics mine*]

There is no reason for the change except as it heightens the meaningfulness of the relationship of priest to boy.

It makes sense that the dead priest, in the boy's dream, should want to confess what he considers to be reprehensible earthly conduct, but the choice of the boy as confessor, entirely lacking in the early versions, is interestingly of a piece with the other late alterations. In the dream the young boy does see himself fleetingly as priest and encourages the confession by his feeble smile. Stephen had, in *A Portrait*, fancied himself in such a role. In *Ulysses* the motif appears also with a cynical tinge when Dedalus, on the beach alone in the Proteus episode, imagines himself a priest and goes through the burlesque motions of a mock Mass. "A garland of grey hair on his comminated head see him me clambering down to the foot pace (*descende*), clutching a monstrance . . . . A choir gives back menace and echo, assisting about the altar's horns . . ." (U 41). And in the same mood of sacrilegious banter, Joyce plays a variation of the theme in *Finnegans Wake* (F 432–433).

The whole dream sequence and its aftermath are complicated additions to the story. To blot out the gray face of the dead priest, the boy tries "to think of Christmas," the birth of Christ. He is not successful in banishing the haunting specter at the time, but, on the next day, the context of the dream is largely dissipated. The boy, in fact, feels guilty that his sadness at the bereavement is not greater. In passages interpolated into the *Dubliners* version, he walks "along the sunny side of the street . . . . I found it strange that neither I nor the day seemed in a mourning mood and I felt even annoyed at discovering in myself a sensation of freedom as if I had been freed from something by his death" (D 11). Several pages further on, the sun image is repeated, "As I walked along in the sun I remembered old Cotter's words . . ." (D 13). The narrator takes the same walk in the *Homestead* story but makes no mention of climatic conditions or of any ambivalence in his attitude toward the old paralytic. The revised weather report seems an attempt to imitate Ibsen's use of naturalistic details of the macrocosm to dramatize the condition of the protagonist's personal world.

By the time the boy takes this walk, he finds it hard to reconstruct "what had happened afterwards in the dream."

> I remembered that I had noticed long velvet curtains and a swinging lamp of antique fashion. I felt that I had been very far away, in some land where the customs were strange – in Persia, I thought . . . . But I could not remember the end of the dream. (D 13)

This typically Yeatsian vision, reminiscent of scenes from two of Yeats's stories which Joyce especially admired – "The Adoration of the Magi" and "The Tables of the Law" – cannot be explained away merely on the basis that Joyce enjoyed putting it in. The curtains of sensuous velvet and the antique lamp are, of course, the trappings of Catholic ornamentation, so that their connection with an Irish cleric or funeral may be justified in that fashion. The faraway land where "the customs were strange," pinpointed to the Middle or Far East by the boy's hunch that it might have been Persia, could just as easily have been the Biblical territory conjured up by his thoughts of Christmas. In *Dubliners*, Joyce attempts to introduce into all the stories capable of holding it this reference to romantic, exotic, distant unreality as a

contrast to the gray drabness of the Dublin scene. The boy
narrator of "An Encounter" goes down to the docks to
examine "the foreign sailors to see had any of them green
eyes for I had some confused notion" (D 25–26). In "Araby"
(and the name of the story is its own motif), Joyce manages
to refer to a nineteenth-century poem called "The Arab's
Farewell to his Steed." The boy in the story finds in the
syllables of the word "Araby" "an Eastern enchantment,"
and he looks "humbly at the great jars that stood like eastern
guards at either side of the dark entrance to the stall . . ."
(D 41). To index all the specific allusions to such exotic
persons, places, and things is unnecessary, but the profusion
of references is strong evidence that addition of the Eastern
dream environment to "The Sisters" was intended by Joyce
as a strengthening of the entire volume rather than for its
restricted meaningfulness in this individual short story.[9]

The same cannot be said for the most important of the
additions to the *Dubliners* version. This half-page, missing
entirely in the *Homestead* story, present to the extent of ten
words in the intermediate manuscript draft, is expanded to
about one hundred and fifty words in the final form:

> We crossed ourselves and came away. In the little room
> downstairs we found Eliza seated in his arm-chair in state. I
> groped my way towards my usual chair in the corner while
> Nannie went to the sideboard and brought out a decanter of
> sherry and some wine-glasses. She set these on the table and
> invited us to take a little glass of wine. Then, at her sister's
> bidding, she filled out the sherry into the glasses and passed
> them to us. She pressed me to take some cream crackers also
> but I declined because I thought I would make too much noise
> eating them. She seemed to be somewhat disappointed at my
> refusal and went over quietly to the sofa where she sat down
> behind her sister. No one spoke: we all gazed at the empty
> fireplace. (D 14–15)

While everyone else sips the wine, the boy hesitates till almost
the end of the story when he waveringly follows the other
guests: "A silence took possession of the little room and, under

cover of it, I approached the table and tasted my sherry and then returned quietly to my chair in the corner." (D 18)

This entire situation, interpolated by the author after August, 1904, seems clearly a dramatic statement of the child's wavering allegiance before the blandishments of the feeble, hard-of-hearing, paralyzed Irish Church. The narrator does not know whether to take or not to take its offerings of Communion, of priesthood. The two sisters, acting as priests, officiate at the ceremony. The boy at first refuses, notices Nannie's disappointment at his refusal, and invents reasons for not complying ("I would make too much noise eating them"). The height of frustration is reached in the scene as "all gazed at the empty fireplace." Embers of spiritual belief are more than cold. They have been removed and nothing is left. Yet the boy, confused, does eventually sip the wine. A few years older in *A Portrait*, Stephen Dedalus knows better how to meet the temptation of female figures who offer him sensuous fruits: "Madam, I never eat muscatel grapes" (P 68).

To reinforce the religious overtones, Joyce adds to the *Dubliners* version other corroborative details not included earlier. When the boy and his aunt come to pay their respects to the dead priest, deaf Nannie, priest-like, leads the way, "her bowed head being scarcely above the level of the banister-rail" (D 13). In the latest draft, the boy is shown as constantly unwilling to continue his association with the clerical household and with things religious. Nannie has to beckon to him "repeatedly with her hand" to get him to enter the "dead-room." Once in the room, they kneel, with Nannie significantly calling the turn, and the prayers commence, "the old woman's mutterings" distracting him. Interestingly, the boy narrator explains that "I pretended to pray but I could not . . ." (D 14). Since this is almost the standard way to portray in literature lost souls in torment – Macbeth the king-killer finds that "Amen" sticks in his throat; the Ancient Mariner cannot pray until he breaks the spell that binds him – it is reasonable to suppose that Joyce added the line to the *Dubliners* draft when he found that the story now reflected his own religious odyssey, that it was no longer merely a character sketch of Father Flynn. That he does finally sip the wine indicates the hold which Ireland and its religious apparatus still have upon him. The artistic consciousness of his position, however, as evidenced by his attempt to make literature out of indecision, shows how far he had come in the year or so since the *Homestead* had carried the original sketch.

It is, of course, possible that Joyce, always eager during these early days for recognition through publication, wrote the *Dubliners* version first, and then admonished by Russell that the *Homestead* would accept only the slightest and most obvious of stories, he expurgated his final draft of all but the naturalistic details of the priest's life in order to submit an acceptable offering. He would then have restored the more subtle motif when he came to prepare *Dubliners* for Grant Richards. I do not myself hold this belief, because it does not accord with Joyce's way of creation by constant elaborating. The process has never been reversible in Joyce's work; the chance that he resorted to expediency here can, I think, be discounted.

There remain to be mentioned several meaningful stylistic changes from draft to draft of "The Sisters." Hugh Kenner has already cited the sharpening of Joyce's point of view, observable in his altering "the ceremonious candles in whose light the Christian must take his last sleep" to the more natural prose rhythms of the boy who tells the story: "I would see the reflection of candles on the darkened blind for I knew that two candles must be set at the head of a corpse"[10] (D 7). Further illustration of the young author's search for the appropriate focus for his narrative is supplied through comparison of the following parallel passages from the three extant drafts:

> *Irish Homestead*: Old Cotter and my uncle were talking at the fire, smoking. Old Cotter is the old distiller who owns the

F

batch of prize setters. He used to be very interesting when I knew him first, talking about 'faints' and 'worms.' Now I find him tedious.

Intermediate manuscript version: Old Cotter and my uncle were talking at the fire, smoking. Old Cotter was a retired distiller who owned a batch of prize setters. He used to be very interesting when I knew him first, talking about 'faints' and 'worms.' Afterwards he became tedious.

Dubliners version: Old Cotter was sitting at the fire, smoking, when I came downstairs to supper. [two paragraphs, not in earlier drafts, are interpolated here] Tiresome old fool! When we knew him first he used to be rather interesting, talking of faints and worms; but I soon grew tired of him and his endless stories about the distillery. (D 7–8)

The first point of interest is the much greater specificity of the early drafts with regard to Cotter's occupation. Impressed more and more by symbolist indirection, Joyce allows the reader to play a progressively larger part in digging out the story. For those, like this reader, unfamiliar with the breeding of dogs, the "faints" and "worms" of the final version call for more effort to comprehend what is being said than do the earlier drafts, which specifically mention "setters." This tendency toward less and less explicitness is general in all of Joyce's stories for which early manuscript versions or serial drafts exist.

The parallel passages which I have reproduced here show also Joyce's uncertainty about the degree of immediacy he ought to impart to his story. The present tense forms of "is" and "owns" in the *Homestead* version, as well as the "the" to designate "batch," place the events of the narrative in the homey present, as though the boy narrator were speaking to "Mangan's sister" down the block on the evening of the priest's death. The batch of setters is taken as familiar to the reader, and Old Cotter assumes the role of neighborhood "character." Apparently fearful that he had become too chatty and personal, Joyce tried in the intermediate manuscript draft to give distance to his narrative through the use of the past tense in these instances, through the substitution of the indefinite article, and through replacing "Now I find him tedious" with the more remote and reflective summary, "Afterwards he became tedious." Though the final version lacks these sentences in their earlier form, so that comparison of specific verbs or articles cannot be made, it retains the distant tone that the intermediate version would lead the reader to expect. This tone makes it possible for Joyce to combine adult insight with childhood experience without abandoning psychological realism.

The *Dubliners* version of the story is much better dramatically than the earlier attempts. Certainly the portrayal of a boy passing through what Ibsen calls a "soul-crisis" is more effectively rendered. Only in the final draft is the reader given an idea of what the boy narrator is like to his elders and of the child's attitude toward them. Just the addition of the single sentence, "I knew that I was under observation so I continued eating as if the news [of Flynn's death] had not interested me," introduces the motif of "silence, exile and cunning" which links the boy to Stephen Dedalus and, by extension, to the reticent author himself. The "apologise-Pull out his eyes" refrain, a juvenile sense of persecution, becomes prominent in the final version as Joyce adds the passage in which Cotter examines the boy with "little beady black eyes," while the child, practicing his *"non serviam"* pose, refuses to "satisfy him by looking up from my plate." Through the boy's uncle John, the reader learns in this final version that the young narrator is averse to exercise and to bathing in cold water, two characteristics, real as well as symbolic, of Stephen Dedalus as a young man. The child's studiousness, his isolation from companions of his own age, his lack of confidence in his foster parents, and the cross-currents of antagonism in the home are all added to the final draft. Their presence gives the reader reason and background for intelligent understanding of what had been earlier merely a stock narrator of a story that did not especially concern him.

By altering the position of certain of the passages in his earlier drafts, Joyce succeeded in improving the dramatic vividness of his story. Both early drafts end with one of the women exclaiming, "God rest his soul!" – a note of positive affirmation upon which this story of frustration, decay, feeble-mindedness, and hopeless lack of progress has no right to end. Joyce must have seen this as he revised, because, though he retains the exhortation as "God have mercy on his soul," he transfers it to the early part of the story and introduces it into the conversation at the dinner table. It is given an ironic twist, too, by its position directly following this speech of the uncle:

> "The youngster and he were great friends. The old chap taught him a great deal, mind you; and they say he had a great wish for him." (D 8)

The ending of the story in the final version thus is allowed to trail off as inconclusively as possible to fit in with the ambiguous position of the boy and the priest: " 'Wide-awake and laughing-like to himself . . . . So then, of course, when they saw that, that made them think that there was something gone wrong with him . . .' " (D 19).

It is necessary to recall here Stanislaus Joyce's insistence that there is nothing directly autobiographical in the stories of *Dubliners*, with the exception of "A Mother" and "An Encounter." To remember his statement is not, however, to forget that those closest to events may be the last to discern the essential verisimilitude of a fictional recreation. It may be that Father Flynn, for instance, does not exist, but the boy narrator, in his relationship to the father figure in "The Sisters," is true to the character of Stephen Dedalus and of Joyce as children. As Joyce told his brother, "There are realities of the imagination too."

Two other sets of changes from draft to draft should be recorded here, one because it shows a significant advance in artistry, the other because its presence is seemingly inexplicable. In the first version (*Homestead*), the coffined priest carries a rosary in his hands. In the intermediate draft, this has been changed and his hands "loosely" retain a cross. The *Dubliners* version describes the motionless figure as holding a chalice. Since, according to the conversation, it was the breaking of the chalice during his life which had caused Father Flynn to lose his firmness of mind and had helped in his physical degeneration, it is quite fitting that Joyce should have altered his text so that the priest could control and hold in death what in life was beyond his powers. The other and more mystifying set of changes would, in another writer, be ascribed to mere frivolousness, but students of Joyce know better than to underestimate his relevant associative powers. When the boy pays a visit, in the *Irish Homestead* draft, to the street on which Flynn lived, he finds, written on a card which is pinned to the funeral wreath on the door, this notice:

July 2nd, 189– The Rev. James Flynn (formerly of St. Ita's Church), aged 65 years. R.I.P.

In the intermediate version, this ostensibly unimportant reference, seemingly an arbitrary designation, has been altered to

July 2nd 1890 The Rev. James Flynn (formerly of S. Catherine's Church, Meath Street) aged sixty-five years. R.I.P.

The *Dubliners* version, finally, shows a different set of statistics:

July 1st, 1895 The Rev. James Flynn (formerly of S. Catherine's Church, Meath Street), aged sixty-five years. R.I.P.

I admit that I do not have the answer to the puzzling alterations. It is possible that there is no logical answer. If Joyce intends identification with his narrator, then the change in date from 1890 to 1895 would alter the age of the boy from eight to thirteen, a more reasonable age for his acting as he does in the story. The fact that thirteen is considered the age of initiation into the mysteries of adulthood may be meaningful. But I have no answer for the change from July 2 to July 1 or for the shift in churches, except that there is a St. Catherine's Church in Dublin, but I have not been able to discover a St. Ita's.

As these pages are being written, a major reconsideration of *Dubliners* by Brewster Ghiselin is appearing serially.[11] Though the author makes no mention of having examined any of the preliminary versions of the stories, his keen analysis of the collection corroborates many of the conclusions previously reached by students of the book and, in addition, goes beyond previous scholarship to suggest "a latent structural unity in *Dubliners*" which Joyce achieves by means of a "highly organized" symbolic framework.

> When the outlines of the symbolic pattern have been grasped, the whole unifying development will be discernible as a sequence of events in a moral drama, an action of the human spirit struggling for survival under peculiar conditions of deprivation, enclosed and disabled by a degenerate environment that provides none of the primary necessities of spiritual life.

Ghiselin devotes attention specifically to the motif of paralysis, the pattern of escape by movement eastward, and the tendency of Joyce to stress "ideas of enclosure." The critic finds that the "unity of *Dubliners* is realized . . . in terms of religious images and ideas, most of them distinctively Christian." He emphasizes the importance to the book of the symbols, sacraments, and doctrines of the Catholic Church, "especially its version of the ancient sacraments of baptism and the sacrificial meal and its concepts of the soul's powers, its perils, and its destiny." As I have tried to do, but with a slightly different emphasis, Ghiselin indicates the presence of the Communion scene in "The Sisters," and gives further significance to the interpolated material of the story by explaining that the uncle's reference to the value of cold baths in childhood suggests baptism. The critic also deals with the oriental motif of several of the stories. Speaking of "The Sisters" and "Araby," he finds that the "far country" referred to in both "is probably the same, that fabulous Arabia which is associated with the Phoenix, symbol of the revewal of life in the resurrection of the sun." Ghiselin's explanation of the dream is logical: "the boy has looked inward toward the source of his own life, away from that civilization which surrounds him but does not sustain him." Elucidating the symbolic motifs of water, color, music, clothing, and others, this article is an intelligent, solidly based attempt to give Joyce's short stories the critical attention they have long deserved.

Joyce's "A Painful Case," the sources and autobiographical implications of which I have already discussed, offers to the student an interesting lesson in literary revision also, for it is, like "The Sisters," available in three versions.[12] The two latest drafts are, however, so much alike that actually the only fruitful comparison is of the earliest with the final published version. Since the second draft is dated in Joyce's hand "15-8-05," it may be presumed that Joyce wrote the story originally during the early or middle months of that year. In the earliest manuscript draft, there is much revision, deletion, marginal addition and elaboration, and, in general, an impression of disorder quite unusual in the ordinarily meticulously handwritten, ostensibly smooth-flowing and uncorrected paragraphs of Joyce's youthful prose manuscripts. In this earliest version, the title is given as "A Painful Incident." The final word is then crossed through and the word "Case" is added. Knowing the care with which Joyce later selected titles for *Ulysses* and *Finnegans Wake*,[13] the reader can see in this early example of seemingly fussy alteration the hand of an artist to whom total relevance in literature was paramount. The original title would have served, it is true, as the headline of the newspaper article announcing Mrs. Sinico's death and could have been used by extension as the name of the story. But Joyce is not presenting merely an incident; the only violent action in the narrative – the accident – is probably the least significant detail to the reader. This story relates, with the bareness of a surgical operating room, a "case" study of the paralysis of emotion in a human being, and in that sense is much broader than the description of an "Incident." Mr. Duffy, moreover, is himself a "case" in the vernacular meaning of that term – a much more painful study than Mrs. Sinico, whose instantaneous death cannot be tragic in the same way that Mr. Duffy's lingering spiritual and human deprivation, willfully self-imposed, is. The caption in the newspaper recording a sudden, violent, and cleanly final happening is presented in ironic contrast to the interminable living death of misguided Mr. Duffy. "A Painful Incident" as title would have been less adequate in establishing the irony. The young writer saw this and quickly took advantage of the broader implications of the ironic second choice.

One meaningful trend that study of the two main drafts of the story reveals is Joyce's very natural reduction in the number of autobiographical references: the attempt, in other words, toward impersonalization. Stanislaus may feel that he himself is characterized in the story as Joyce thought his brother would become in later life; he may insist that Joyce "drew little from himself because he had reason not to consider himself a good type of celibate."[14] The reader of all Joyce's works, however, must feel that Duffy is, perhaps more than his author wants him to be, a portrait of the writer. Citation of several examples of discarded lines from the story, which help to identify Joyce with Duffy, is in order here.

This is a passage from the early draft:

> He asked himself what else could he have done – carried on a comedy of furtive comedy which must have ended in mutual disgust or gone away with her out of Ireland. Either course would have been ridiculous. He thought of the pain impossible the one an undignified intrigue the other a ridiculous elopement. He had acted for the best . . . .

This is the parallel passage from *Dubliners*:

> He asked himself what else could he have done. He could not have carried on a comedy of deception with her; he could not have lived with her openly. He had done what seemed to him best . . . . (D 145)

Since Joyce wrote this story just a few months at best after eloping with Nora Barnacle from Ireland, just a few months after his jeering college pals and head-shaking elders had branded the alliance ridiculous and insisted that Joyce would be back soon, and alone, his inclusion in the original story of these very personal details is a clue to the manner in which he conceived the protagonist.[15] At still another point in the early version of "A Painful Case," the young writer of epiphanies, who was at that moment preparing a volume of short stories, added a profuse marginal interpolation, part of which contained the fragment: "Every two or three days he ~~added~~ composed a short sentence ~~to an unwritten story~~ containing a subject in the third person and a predicate in the past tense. ~~This odd habit grew on him unawares.~~" It is worth noting that Joyce deleted all mention of Duffy as a writer of short stories from the final draft. Though other citations might be adduced to reinforce my point, I think that no further examples are necessary.

The heavily revised early manuscript draft of "A Painful Case" offers especially useful insights into Joyce's method of composition. The first paragraph of the newspaper article that informs Duffy of his unfortunate friend's death, gives the impression of a writer intensely concerned with the tools of his trade – the words of the language – trying almost desperately to achieve Flaubert's aim of the exact adjective or verb needed to present his point in precisely the correct perspective. Since this newspaper article in the story is intended to simulate the dead matter-of-factness of mediocre journalistic prose – a level approached by all the Dublin papers of the time that I have examined – one might think that Joyce's painstaking efforts could have been saved for passages more worthy of artistic care. The passage reads this way:

> ~~This~~ Today at the Morgue ~~the Mr Levret~~ the deputy Coroner in the absence of Mr Levret held an inquest on the body of Mrs Emily Sinico [caret] aged 42 years, [end caret] ~~of Leoville Merrion~~ who ~~was killed was knocked down died~~ was killed ~~by in the accident~~ at Sydney Parade Station ~~last~~ on yesterday evening ~~Tuesday last.~~ The evidence showed that the deceased lady ~~travelled from Westland Row~~ while attempting to cross the line was knocked down by the buffer of the engine . . . . (D 141)

Some of the changes are apparently arbitrary, for the paragraph would seem to be just as effective newspaper prose with or without the alterations. Others seem designed to make details of the accident correspond closely with standard procedure that would operate in Dublin in such an event. In this paragraph and elsewhere in the article, the author changes names of people and places, alters ages, times of day, and other specific items of information as if in anticipation of the Thom's *Directory* approach which characterizes the later *Ulysses*. The less interesting second draft of the story, which I have already mentioned, differs from the first version mainly, indeed, in its alterations of the names of minor characters and ostensibly unimportant places. Thus, the "Morgue" of the excerpt quoted above becomes in that version "Vincent's Hospital," which in turn becomes, in the *Dubliners* story, "the City of Dublin Hospital." Even the name of the assistant house surgeon who examines the dead woman is altered from "Dr. Cosgrove" to "Dr. Halpin." Most peculiar of all these mysterious changes, yet explicable perhaps in terms of Joyce's fascination with correspondences and magic numbers and birthdays, is the constantly shifting badge number of the constable who corroborates the evidence given by Police Sergeant Croly. The officer is represented in the story by the three words : "Constable 57E corroborated."

This brief and colorless appearance hardly justifies deliberate care in the assigning of the man's number; yet, in various stages of revision, the constable is designated as "42D," "47D," "57D," and finally, in the published story, "57E." Maybe, in the absence of a reasonable explanation, it is better to ascribe such alterations to the whims of a young man with a pen in his hand.

As a final example of the revision that "A Painful Case" underwent before publication, I should like to offer two rather extensive parallel passages, one from the early draft and the other from the published version. These excerpts comprise most of page 146 in the Modern Library edition. The early draft reads this way:

He was alone in through the deserted alleys where they had walked four years ago and it seemed to him that he was not alone. At moments in the stillness her voice seem [*sic*] to touched his ear to and he stood still to listen. He had held her life withheld life from her, said Why had he withheld life from her. Why had he sentenced her to death? He felt his morality falling to pieces.

As he passed over the Magazine Hill he looked along the river towards the city, the lights of which seemed ["to him now" is written in the margin] all that was human and hospitable in the "august inhospitable, inhuman night." There they had been born. In the shadow of the Park wall he saw some human figures lying. He could not frame an angry thought that the sight of those squ furtive or venal loves filled him with despair.

He forgot that he had lived a life of unbroken rectitude, and remembered only that he had lived the life of an one outcast from life's feast. One person human being alone had seemed to love him and he had sentenced her to death, a shameful death. He had withheld life and happiness from her. He stood on the crest of the hill and gazed again at the smooth gleaming river and at the figures lying in the shadow of the wall. Beyond the river he saw a long ["goods" is written in the margin for interpolation here] train creeping out of Kingsbridge Station. It crept out slowly like a worm with a fiery head labouring laboriously and ~~slowly~~ obstinately. He watched it creep slowly out of sight and in his ears he still heard the laborious melody of the engine.

"Émily Śinico, Émily Śinico, Émily Śinico."

He turned back . . . .

The same passage, as refined and improved for inclusion in *Dubliners*, follows:

He walked through the bleak alleys where they had walked four years before. She seemed to be near him in the darkness. At moments he seemed to feel her voice touch his ear, her hand touch his. He stood still to listen. Why had he withheld life from her? Why had he sentenced her to death? He felt his moral nature falling to pieces.

When he gained the crest of the Magazine Hill he halted and looked along the river towards Dublin, the lights of which burned redly and hospitably in the cold night. He looked down the slope and, at the base, in the shadow of the wall of the Park, he saw some human figures lying. Those venal and furtive loves filled him with despair. He gnawed the rectitude of his life; he felt that he had been outcast from life's feast. One human being had seemed to love him and he had denied her life and happiness: he had sentenced her to ignominy, a death of shame. He knew that the prostrate creatures down by the wall were watching him and wished him gone. No one wanted him; he was outcast from life's feast. He turned his eyes to the grey gleaming river, winding along towards Dublin. Beyond the river he saw a goods train winding out of Kingsbridge Station, like a worm with a fiery head winding through the darkness, obstinately and laboriously. It passed slowly out of sight; but still he heard in his ears the laborious drone of the engine (reiterating the syllables of her name.)

He turned back . . . .

The principle behind some of the alterations is rather obvious. The total number of lines is reduced from thirty-five to twenty-seven (actually to twenty-nine or thirty, if we do not count the crossed-out passages), a loss of one-seventh of the original words in the normal process of economizing on superfluous phrases. The same tendency shows Joyce resisting the influence of Pater's hypnotically gushing sentences, as he substitutes for the purple and agonizingly personal wordiness of "all that was human and hospitable in the 'august inhospitable, inhuman night' " the simpler and more effective line, "the lights of which burned redly and hospitably in the cold night." Other changes, like the substitution of "before" for "ago" in the first sentence of each excerpt, repeat the author's tendency, pointed out in "The Sisters," to give distance and objectivity to his narrative by making the point of view less immediate.

Several of the alterations, however, are much more subtle and give evidence of a remarkable growth of artistic power in the short time which separates the two versions of the story. Throughout the narrative of Mr. Duffy, there runs the motif of eating and drinking – what Mr. Ghiselin would call, perhaps, overtones of the sacrificial meal. Duffy whimsically records "the headline of an advertisement for *Bile Beans*." His desk exudes the fragrance of an overripe apple. Living his spiritual life "without any communion with others," he follows an undeviating ritual of barren and sterile communion with himself as he daily takes his lunch, "a bottle of lager beer and a small trayful of arrowroot biscuits," in a pub, and his dinner at another restaurant, again in solitude, "where he felt himself safe from the society of Dublin's gilded youth" (D 135). Joyce says nothing of this soulless ritual during the time of Duffy's relationship with Mrs. Sinico. Perhaps the protagonist is able to find, in a relationship with another human being who "became his confessor," a substitute for the mechanical motions of daily ingestion, for the husk of communion with self lacking the kernel of emotional satisfaction. With the banishment of his female confessor, the repudiation of the sole link which Duffy has had with life and love, and therefore with spiritual ease, he returns to his round of unsatisfactory eating: "And still every morning he went into the city by tram and every evening walked home from the city after having dined moderately in George's Street and read the evening paper for dessert" (D 140). Perhaps significantly, it is during his occupation with this activity that he gets his just desserts – his knowledge of the "DEATH OF A LADY AT SYDNEY PARADE," the painful case in which he is so deeply involved. This heavy blow, the first revelation to him of his crimes of omission, falls as he is "about to put a morsel of corned beef and cabbage into his mouth." The very length of this descriptive aside placed prominently in the first sentence of the paragraph testifies to its importance in Joyce's mind. At this most crucial moment of the story, Joyce insists on a slow-motion carrying out of Duffy's accustomed ritual even in the face of an overwhelming discovery. Duffy "replaced the morsel of food on his plate and read the paragraph attentively. Then he drank a glass of water, pushed his plate to one side, doubled the paper down before him between his elbows and read the paragraph over and over again." The first effects of the permanent loss of his confessor, the person who had offered him a moment of life which he had abruptly rejected, are observable in the break in the ritual, the spoiling of the food on the table. "The cabbage began to deposit a cold white grease on his plate." More than that, however, he can no longer find any comfort even in this ersatz nourishment:

> The girl came over to him to ask was his dinner not properly cooked. He said it was very good and ate a few mouthfuls of it with difficulty. Then he paid his bill and went out (D 140).

It is neither his heart nor his soul that is distressed by the awful death of Mrs. Sinico – but his digestive apparatus. "The threadbare phrases, the inane expressions of sympathy, the cautious words of a reporter won over to conceal the details of a commonplace vulgar death attacked his stomach" (D 144). In a public house at Chapelizod Bridge, Duffy has great difficulty in downing one glass of hot punch, though "five or six workingmen," in friendly and jovial communion with one another, have no trouble in drinking the contents of "their huge pint tumblers." His moral upset is made concrete in terms of food and drink.

With this background, it is interesting to return to a comparison of the two drafts of "A Painful Case." Duffy's epiphany of self-knowledge, his moment of understanding of the meaning of his life, when it comes, should be clothed ideally in the metaphor of food, of the stomach. In the early draft, Joyce is only partially successful as he has Mr. Duffy forgetting "that he had lived a life of unbroken rectitude, and [remembering] . . . only that he had lived the life of an one outcast from life's feast." By the time Joyce was ready to do the final draft, he repeats the "life's feast" section twice; also the whole sentence is all of a piece, the metaphor brilliantly executed: "He gnawed the rectitude of his life; he felt that he had been outcast from life's feast." Deprived through his moral paralysis and emotional stultification of further satisfaction in his solitary ritual of eating, as he watches the "venal and furtive loves" about him, his bitter sustenance is the memory of the misguided rules by which he has lived. That these memories must be "gnawed" rather than thought about is a thoroughly worth-while artistic retribution of which the younger Joyce had not been capable. The culmination of the motif is still to come, however, at the end of the paragraph.

Though Mr. Duffy feels lonely and rejected, there has been, up until the end of the paragraph, no real, dramatic act of rejection, no attempt to objectify the internal situation. The early draft makes a beginning in this direction. Duffy gazes at the "smooth gleaming river and at the figures lying in the shadow of the wall." Then he sees a train, which he changes to a "goods train" in the same draft, slowly crawling like a worm out of the station. The rhythmic noise of its engine seems to say "Emily Sínico" over and over again until the train disappears. On the symbolic as on the real level, this panoramic view of Duffy's lost opportunity, against a backdrop of furtive love-making, is effective. The river, which in the final version winds "along towards Dublin," is the female principle – the watery wife, Anna Livia Plurabelle, of *Finnegans Wake*. The train, male and worm like, follows a path roughly paralleling that of the river without the chance, ever, of communion with it. In Duffy's deliberate and plodding way, it "obstinately and laboriously" winds through, meaningfully, "the darkness." Like Duffy, it had been, as Ghiselin points out, the instrument of the woman's death. Joyce evidently felt, between the time of the first and the final draft, that he had been too explicit and obvious in ascribing to the noise of the engine the "Emily Sinico" refrain, so that in the published story this has been muted to the less direct "reiterating the syllables of her name.".... In seeing this bit of naturalistic Dublin landscape, however, Duffy becomes fully aware of his emotional plight. "He felt that he was alone" (D 147).

Because the early drafts of the stories of *Dubliners* have been, until recently, inaccessible even to scholars, the richness of insight that they offer into the work of a remarkable craftsman has not been recognized. Only Hugh Kenner has used the preliminary versions at all, and he has used them quite incidentally. Though I shall not attempt here any further detailed analysis of changes made, for instance, in successive manuscripts of "The Boarding House" or of "Eveline," it is important to point out that such materials for research exist and reward patient examination by biographers or students of the modern short story.

The broad differences between *Stephen Hero* and *A Portrait of the Artist as a Young Man* have been so frequently pointed out that they are critical commonplaces by this time. Editing the two hundred odd pages that remain extant of the voluminous first draft of Joyce's novel of adolescence, Theodore Spencer indicated in his Introduction the chief points of difference: the drastic cutting of the *Portrait* so that it contains only about one-fifth the bulk of the original draft; the omission of many scenes which originally had a place in the story and the consequent dropping out or cutting down of parts assigned to minor characters; the alteration in tone and focus from the

G

"far more direct and less elliptical form" of *Stephen Hero* to the poetic and suggestively hazy outlines of *A Portrait*; finally, Joyce's moving from frankly polemical, expository presentation of his environment, almost in essay fashion, to an impressionist technique and a symbolic approach.[1] Somewhat later, Joseph Prescott, taking advantage of Spencer's invitation to "every reader" to go beyond general considerations to detailed and "exhaustive comparisons," pointed out specific instances in which careful reading of the fragmentary early draft could illuminate difficult spots in *Ulysses* and other of Joyce's works.[2]

More recently, in an unpublished Master's Thesis, Philip L. Handler has subjected both drafts of *A Portrait* to extensive and fruitful comparison.[3] Handler's most important general contribution is his conclusion, based on painstaking analysis of both versions, that, though Joyce may evolve his aesthetic theory in *Stephen Hero*, he does not apply it "until the writing of the *Portrait*." It was not until Joyce was able to supplant "autobiography, the impure lyric novel," by "the only valid kind of novel, the dramatic one," that *A Portrait* emerged as a truly original work of art. Because Mr. Handler's work is available in the Columbia University Library, I shall confine myself to discussing only those aspects of comparison that have not been treated by him or by others.

The principal value of *Stephen Hero* is that it not only enables us to penetrate Joyce's mind during the years when *Dubliners* was being written, but also affords us insights into his finished *Portrait* and even into his later books. Thought out and composed at the most tempestuous period, intellectually and emotionally, of the artist's life – the crucial years which saw his decision to leave the Church, go into exile from Ireland, turn to writing as a career, marry, adopt a style – this manuscript reflects the pull of forces exerted upon the frail young man hardly out of his adolescence. And because it is the most strictly autobiographical document which Joyce wrote, it allows the student to assess the information of the stories and of the later novels as works that mirror or distort the actual qualities of their author. Joyce's increasingly complex presentation, often in subversive symbolic form, may be understood and enjoyed through the use of the *Stephen Hero* manuscript as a kind of bald, prosaic commentary on the works of shadowy intent which are nearly contemporaneous with it.

The operation of this measuring rod may be illustrated by reference to Joyce's short story entitled "Grace." Though I shall save extensive analysis of this story for my final chapter, I should like at this point merely to approach its underlying structure through recourse to *Stephen Hero*. Even though one may never have heard Stanislaus Joyce's remark that in "Grace" his brother intended a rough parody of the *Divine Comedy*,[4] the reader would probably have noticed the threefold division of the story, unusual in *Dubliners*, and the position of the protagonist, Tom Kernan, in each of the three sections: face down on the floor of a lavatory in a pub; then in bed in his own middle-class home, surrounded by friends whose plan it is to improve him through the improvement of his religious status; and finally among the congregation of the highly respected Jesuit church on Gardiner Street. This steady rise upward from filth to good fortune, in three well-defined steps, occurring in an environment of small talk about faith, religion, papal powers, and the like, may easily have caused readers familiar with Joyce's love of literary analogies to suspect the presence of Dante's poem in a story with a name like "Grace."

At this point, familiarity with *Stephen Hero* helps a great deal, helps more, it may be said, than equal acquaintance with the less informative *Portrait*. First, the manuscript draft is full of references to Dante, if any evidence is required that Joyce knew the Italian poet. Stephen Daedalus's sessions learning Italian with Father Artifoni are described at some length. Much more pertinent, however, is a passage which presents the autobiographical figure of Stephen Daedalus actually planning to write such a story as "Grace" or "Ivy Day in the Committee Room," both heavy with Dantean condemnation of the contemporary scene:

> The ugly artificiality of the lives over which Father Healy was comfortably presiding struck this outrageous instant out of him and he went on repeating to himself a line from Dante for no other reason except that it contained the angry disyllable "frode." Surely, he thought, I have as much right to use the word as ever Dante had. The spirits of Moynihan and O'Neill and Glynn seemed to him worthy of some blowing about round the verges of a hell which would be a caricature of Dante's. The spirits of the patriotic and religious enthusiasts seemed to him fit to inhabit the fraudulent circles where hidden in hives of immaculate ice they might work their bodies to the due pitch of frenzy. The spirits of the tame sodalists, unsullied and undeserving, he would petrify amid a ring of Jesuits in the circle of foolish and grotesque virginities and ascend above them and their baffled icons to where his Emma, with no detail of her earthly form or vesture abated, invoked him from a Mohammadan paradise. (S 158–159)

In "Ivy Day," as the fire burns redly in the room and the ambiguous Father Keon comes to speak to the political treasurer, the "patriotic" enthusiasts are caricatured in a Dantean scene. In "Grace," it is the turn of the "religious enthusiasts" to "inhabit the fraudulent circles" and to be petrified "amid a ring of Jesuits."

The gloss of *Stephen Hero* does more, however, than help to confirm the presence of Dantean structure in "Grace." It presents the young author's feelings about the condition of religious life in his Ireland – feelings which he dramatizes in more than one of the stories. The dominant imagery of the business world, summed up in Father Purdon's "text for business men" and his hope that each man would be his own "spiritual accountant," receives scathing notice in the manuscript version: "He [Stephen] said to Cranly that the chapel with its polished benches and incandescent lamps reminded him of an insurance office" (S 118).

Stephen visits the same Gardiner Street church in *Stephen Hero* to find the chapel "crowded from altar to doors with a well-dressed multitude."

> Everywhere he saw the same flattered affection for the Jesuits who are in the habit of attaching to their order the souls of thousands of the insecurely respectable middle-class by offering them a refined asylum, an interested, a considerate confessional, a particular amiableness of manners which their spiritual adventures in no way entitled them to. (S 119–120)

If there is any doubt about the narrator's position in "Grace," it is effectively dispelled by recourse to the corroborative lines of the autobiographical novel.

Further perusal of allusions to Dante in *Stephen Hero* supplies Joyce's rationale for the ironic note which is struck in *Dubliners* whenever the author attempts to portray human love. The young protagonist's reading of the *Vita Nuova* gives him the notion of gathering his "scattered love-verses into a perfect wreath," but such a project presents difficulties that did not trouble the bards of Dante's world. Stephen complains that

> in his expressions of love he found himself compelled to use what he called the feudal terminology and as he could not use it with his same faith and purpose as animated the feudal poets themselves he was compelled to express his love a little ironically. This suggestion of relativity, he said, mingling itself with so immune a passion is a modern note: we cannot swear or expect eternal fealty because we recognise too accurately the limits of every human energy. It is not possible for the modern lover to think the universe an assistant at his love-affair . . . .
> (S 174)

It is not surprising, therefore, that when the narrator of "Araby" reaches the bazaar – the goal of his quest for love and romance – "the light was out" or that a flippant salesgirl is sufficiently menacing to the modern lover to prevent him from carrying out his mission. Not only is the meaning of "Araby" made clearer by Stephen's pronouncement on aesthetics, but the place of love in all Joyce's books is illuminated.

Permeated by the religion that he sought to reject, Joyce's mind considered and reconsidered during the early years of this century the impotent state into which he felt the Church had lapsed. Many evidences of this psychological struggle find their way into *Stephen Hero* and, of course, into the stories of *Dubliners*. While there is no difficulty in dating the stories quite precisely, thanks to Joyce's habit of appending the date of completion to his manuscript drafts[5] and to his frequent announcements in letters to Grant Richards[6] that he has finished this or that story on a certain day, it is hard to tell whether many of the stories were written before or after sections of *Stephen Hero* that bear directly on them. Scholars vary in their estimates of the time Joyce spent on his autobiographical novel. Joseph Prescott puts the date of beginning at 1901, Sylvia Beach at 1903, and Herbert Gorman, quoting Joyce, at 1904.[7] All agree that by 1906 Joyce had completed everything that he was to do on the manuscript and had turned his attention to *A Portrait*. If Professor Prescott is right – and the generality of published opinion has come around to his way of thinking – then probably the statements on religion in *Stephen Hero* antedate the dramatization of similar sentiments in stories like "The Sisters" and "Grace." Once more, then, the student may turn to relevant passages in the earlier work to gloss the later.

In this connection, Stephen's revulsion at the paralyzing effects of Irish religion is meaningful as applied to the imagery of "The Sisters":

> These wanderings filled him [Stephen] with deep-seated anger and whenever he encountered a burly black-vested priest taking a stroll of pleasant inspection through these warrens full of swarming and cringing believers he cursed the farce of Irish Catholicism: an island . . . the inhabitants of which entrust their wills and minds to others that they may ensure for themselves a life of *spiritual paralysis* [Italics mine] . . . . (S 146)

Once more, describing the "deadly chill" in the atmosphere of his Catholic college, he attributes to it his "paralysed . . . heart" (S 194). Musing on the "plague of Catholicism," he envisages "the vermin begotten in the catacombs in an age of sickness . . . issuing forth upon the plains and mountains of Europe. . . . They obscured the sun. Contempt of [the body] human nature, weakness, nervous tremblings, fear of day and job, distrust of man and life . . . beset the body burdened and disaffected in its members by its black tyrannous lice" (S 194). The seeds of the relationship between Father Flynn and the boy narrator of "The Sisters" seem to be germinating here. The black-clad priest, paralyzed and feeble, exercises a power over the physically weak lad, who does not go in for healthful athletics or cold baths. The priest dies at night, but after his death the darkness that had hitherto "obscured the sun" seems dissipated, and Joyce refers to bright sunlight and the feeling of freedom and relief that comes to the boy with Flynn's demise. "Exultation of the mind before joyful beauty, exultation of the body in free confederate labours, every natural impulse towards health and wisdom and happiness had been corroded by the pest of these vermin" (S 194) but, it should be assumed from the story, would be restored following the final removal of the cause.

In other places in *Stephen Hero*, Joyce inadvertently alludes to situations analogous to those presented in the story of Father Flynn in terminology so distinctly parallel that he reveals more than he intends of the true motives behind his story façade. Writing of Stephen's attitude toward women, Joyce says:

> He cursed her burgher cowardice and her beauty and he said to himself that though her eyes might cajole *the half-witted God of the Roman Catholics* they would not cajole him. (S 210)

The temptation is great to recall the description of Father Flynn who, after his accident with the chalice ("That affected his mind"), "began to mope by himself, talking to no one and wandering about by himself." He sinks into an even more serious condition, "wide-awake and laughing-like to himself . . . that made them think that there was something gone wrong with him . . ." (D 18–19). An even more conclusive example of inescapable analogy is offered by comparison of the boy narrator's remark on Flynn's demeanor in accepting gifts (simony?) and, couched in nearly identical phraseology in *Stephen Hero*, Stephen's observation on a similar situation. In "The Sisters," the sentence reads,

> Perhaps my aunt would have given me a packet of High Toast for him and this present would have *roused him from his stupefied doze*. (D 11)

The parallel passage in *Stephen Hero* puts it this way:

> He entered the Church in Gardiner St and, passing by without honouring the table of the lay-brother who *roused himself from a stupefied doze* in expectation of silver, arrived in the right wing of the chapel. (S 119)

Consideration of the parallel passages, which I have italicized, indicates without question that, in Joyce's mind at least, the story of Father Flynn has symbolic values and that the paralyzed figure represents a much larger area of meaning than is explicit in his superficial role.

On matters of smut and perversion Joyce writes with a straightforwardness of pattern most interesting to follow from book to book. Adhering to Platonic doctrine, Joyce makes his unsavory characters always look the part. In "An Encounter," the old pervert, in his shabby greenish-black suit and high hat, stares at the boys with "bottle-green eyes peering . . . from under a twitching forehead" (D 31). In *Stephen Hero*, Moynihan, representative in the novel of Dublin's soiled and smutty approach to sexual matters – sanctioned and respectable, Stephen points out, though his own honest and open views on sex are met with horrified displeasure – is made to carry physically the marks of his twisted psychological set:

> He was an extremely [small] [the bracket is Joyce's] ugly young man with a wide mouth which gave the idea that it was under his chin until the face was seen at close quarters, eyes of an over-washed olive green colour set viciously close together, and large rigid ears standing far apart . . . . Moynihan . . . said he would like to know Italian on account of Boccaccio and the other Italian writers. He told Stephen that if he wanted to read something 'smutty' . . . the *Decameron* took the biscuit for 'smut.' (S 149–150)

Commenting on Stephen's good fortune in being a student of Italian, Moynihan goes on:

> – I wish I was like you . . . it must be ten times as bad in the original. I can't tell you now because here's my tram . . . but it takes the biscuit for downright . . . [ellipsis marks are Joyce's] you know? (S 149–150)

Though Moynihan plays a much larger role in *A Portrait*, the reader discovers there only that this boorish young man is consistently dirty in mind and speech, "snoutish" in appearance.

There is in *A Portrait* a short and apparently inexplicable scene in which an alleged pervert is introduced (P 267–268), a man of "dwarfish stature . . . . Under the dome of his tiny hat his unshaven face began to smile with pleasure and he was heard to murmur." He has a "monkeyish face" and his mouth, speaking with "gentle pleasure," talks purringly. Cranly supplies the information that "the captain has only one love: sir Walter Scott," while another young man asks him, "What are your reading now, captain? . . . – *The Bride of Lammermoor?*"

> – I love old Scott – the flexible lips said – I think he writes something lovely. There is no writer can touch sir Walter Scott. –

As Stephen listens, he admires the "genteel accent, low and

moist, marred by errors: and, listening to it, he wondered was the story true and was the thin blood that flowed in his shrunken frame noble and come of an incestuous love?"

Those who have examined carefully the description of the captain here and compared it with that of the "old josser" in *Dubliners* do not need to be reminded of striking similarities: both old men meet Stephen and his closest friend (Mahony in one book, Cranly in the other); the pervert in the short story "said he had all Sir Walter Scott's works . . . and never tired of reading them" (D 28). Both men smile continually. Both speak in a low, hypnotizing voice, repeating their "phrases over and over again, varying them and surrounding them with . . . [their] monotonous voice" (D 29). The eyes of one peer "from under a twitching forehead," while, for the other, "his thin quick eyelids beat often over his sad eyes." From all these similarities, it should be apparent that Joyce, economical as usual with the treasury of usable literary material in his notebook storehouses, altered a few details, descriptive and narrative, but put to use essentially his stock characterization of the abnormal male personality in books written at different times. And the figure of Moynihan, too, with his small stature, ugly face, green eyes, and references to authors of risqué novels and stories, shares many of the attributes of Joyce's stereotype.

The introduction of the pervert in "An Encounter" is necessary to the story and gives the narrative both its manifest and its symbolic point and climax. In *A Portrait*, on the other hand, there seems to be no reason on any level why "the captain" must be brought in. He has no active part in the narrative. He appears in only one short scene, covering little more than a full page. He reveals to us no information concerning the protagonist or any other main character in the novel. Yet he is there because this is an impressionist book and he has impressed Stephen sufficiently to have a niche in the young man's portrait gallery. He is used to supply Stephen with a series of thoughts that he would not, under other circumstances, have entertained but whose presence in the book is essential to a revelation of secret places in the boy's consciousness. "He frowned angrily upon his thought and on the shrivelled mannikin who had called it forth" (P 269).

To illustrate Joyce's new artistic use of the old pervert-figure, I must quote the rather long paragraph which follows directly, with no transition whatever, Stephen's speculation as to whether the old man had really descended from a noble and incestuous line:

> The park trees were heavy with rain and rain fell still and ever in the lake, lying grey like a shield. A game of swans flew there and the water and the shore beneath were fouled with their greenwhite slime. They embraced softly impelled by the grey rainy light, the wet silent trees, the shield like witnessing lake, the swans. They embraced without joy or passion, his arm wrapped around his sister's neck. A grey woolen cloak was wrapped athwart her from her shoulder to her waist: and her fair head was bent in willing shame. He had loose redbrown hair and tender shapely strong freckled hands. Face? There was no face seen. The brother's face was bent upon her fair rain fragrant hair. The hand freckled and strong and shapely and caressing was Davin's hand. (P 268)

Annoyed with these thoughts, "he held them at a distance and brooded uneasily . . . . Why were they not Cranly's hands? Had Davin's simplicity and innocence stung him more secretly?" And that is all.

With Stephen's thoughts in seemingly chaotic riot, the reader suddenly finds himself outside the library and in St. Stephen's Park watching swans pollute the lake. The deliberately ambiguous reference of pronouns, intended to afford the reader an exercise in grammatical gymnastics somewhat akin to the train of stampeding memories in the protagonist, first assigns the "they" in the next line logically to "swans." Then, fortified by the information in the next sentence concerning the nature of the embrace, the reader transfers the reference to members of the captain's incestuous family, thus providing the bridge which the author intended between the two apparently discrete paragraphs. The description of the "he," however, so utterly at odds with what we know of the old man's creature-like appearance, offers impetus to the reader for hurried reconsideration. Perhaps the "she" is Stephen's girl. Joyce tantalizes his audience by withholding to the end of the paragraph any definite identification. "There was," as he puts it, "no face seen." Finally the hand is identified as "Davin's," a most unexpected outcome for the reader, who had been prepared by the author to equate the figure of the country lad with innocence and rather naïve cleanliness. Following a parallel train of thought, Stephen also feels that the attribution of guilt has been directed against the wrong man, and even accuses himself of evil thoughts engendered by jealousy that another human being could maintain simple integrity in the Dublin environment.

If Joyce seeks, in this paragraph, to question the honest and wholesome sanctity of love in the Irish atmosphere at the turn of the century, he is certainly successful. Like the portraits which melt into one another in *Finnegans Wake*, here the good and the bad, the just and the unjust, merge nebulously in a medley of jumbled but far from random impressions. The sharp picture of perversion dramatized is merely the prelude to a view of a mind on the brink of damnation, that can turn beauty into ugliness and see the straight as crooked. The swans – the symbol, as birds, of flight, of beauty, and, in Joyce's words, of "things of the intellect" – here fly down, not away, and are seen in an ugly, gray light as they foul their surroundings with "greenwhite" slime. Even the colour of perversion, as reported in the eyes of Moynihan and the old man of "An Encounter," is repeated. That Stephen is capable here of believing the worst of Cranly or of Davin and, by implication, of Emma as representative of all women, is evidence of the low state of his spiritual resources at this point. Love of country, of family, of Church – all these have turned sour and, for whatever reason, have been perverted to empty and meaningless rituals. It is perhaps significant that Stephen should turn at this point – directly after connecting Cranly with the evil vision in the park – to an ostensibly intellectual discussion with his college peers under the colonnade of the library, the center of learning in Dublin, and that here too the environment should be polluted. What Stephen prizes above all else now – all that is left to him – does not rise above the level of parody (the genealogy of the Forster family) (P 270) and drunken banter:

> – Tell us, Temple – O'Keeffe said – how many quarts of porter have you in you? –
> – All your intellectual soul is in that phrase, O'Keeffe – said Temple with open scorn. (P 269)

Stripped one by one of all the prizes of life that mean anything to him, Stephen finds it high time to save himself from drowning in the green slime and entwining seaweed of a sea of perverted hopes (as Dilly is fated to do in *Ulysses*), and he gets out.

A few final remarks on the epiphany of the captain's background of perversion and on its accompanying swan-incest paragraph will suffice. That the incident is indeed an epiphany is clear to anyone who studies the pattern of the twenty-odd unpublished notebook jottings known as the Epiphanies. That it has the effect on Stephen which Joyce hoped his epiphanies would have on literary audiences is also clear, for it illuminates, in a flash of dramatized existence, the meaning of a whole group of seemingly unrelated phenomena in the protagonist's life. We do not know whether the young man's thoughts, in the "swan" paragraph, are thoughts only – or whether the meeting at the bridge ever took place. We do not know which of his friends, if any, were involved. Nor does it matter, any more than it matters in *Ulysses* whether Stephen actually calls upon his Aunt Sara or whether he simply lives the scene which imagination develops. The events of the paragraph, real or imagined, have just as much life if Stephen's mind organizes them as if everyday circumstances cause them to happen. When the mind is Joyce's, perhaps they have more.

A prime illustration of Joyce's way of borrowing is provided by his handling of the fire-lighting scene during which the dean of the college converses with Stephen. J. F. Byrne, calling on scholars, in a sarcastic exhortation, to examine the incident for hidden meanings, indignantly calls it a "conglomeration of piffle" and claims credit for it as the actual student involved in the interview with the dean. He explains how, seven years after the episode had occurred, he "committed the blunder of telling Joyce about this incident" in 1902, and how he later regretted doing so when he saw how Joyce "abused" the story.[8] Even more unforgivable to Byrne is that the distortion is not the result of the author's misunderstanding of the event or even a partial failure of memory with the passing of the years, for in *Stephen Hero*, says Byrne, the episode had originally been dramatized by Joyce "with approximate accuracy in fewer than two hundred words." The scene required no more elaboration than that, Byrne feels, because very little actually happened. Father Darlington (the Father Butt of *Stephen Hero*) entered the room, greeted Byrne, hesitated several times, finally prepared to light the fire, lit it, and, pleased with his own technique, exclaimed, " 'Pon my word, Mister – Mister Byrne, there's quite an art in lighting a fire, is there not!" Byrne agreed. Both men caught sight of a pretty coed outside the window and the priest commented on her attractiveness. Then, with a smile, the old man left the room, ending the interview. From this, Byrne complains, Joyce manufactured tundishes, aesthetics, and an intellectual battle of minds – all pure invention.

I think that we may accept Byrne's version as correct here and agree that the incident was blown up by the author beyond all proportion. The adaptable young Joyce has more than once been accused of the same crime by other annoyed and literal-minded eyewitnesses. These well-meaning literalists, however, forget that the writer of a novel – especially of a symbolic-impressionist novel – has an obligation to tell a deeper truth than is involved in faithful repetition of the manifest details of a situation. What may appear to be distortion and misapplication of "facts," under the skillful hands of the artist, may result in illumination of character. What might have happened may be more revelatory than what did happen. It is significant that in *Stephen Hero*, more autobiographical and less contrived artistically, though Joyce introduces the fire-lighting scene as his own, he does not alter the other facts substantially. By the time of *A Portrait*, whatever had belonged to Byrne had been submerged and Stephen Dedalus is in full command.

The changes are impressive. From a vignette of twenty-two lines in the earlier version, the incident is given a full eight pages in *A Portrait*. Many of the ingredients of the long colloquy in the later novel are scattered here and there throughout *Stephen Hero* but are not fused and given dramatic continuity by presentation in one episode. References to meaning of words like "detail," for instance, are made in one meeting of Stephen with Father Butt, while the fire-lighting takes place during a different meeting. Furthermore, in the earlier book the discussion of the meaning of certain words comes before the lighting of the fire; in the later book it follows as a consequence of the fire-lighting. Stephen's use of Aquinas's *"Pulcra sunt quae visa placent"* definition in *Stephen Hero*, comes in his dialogue with the President of the college. In *A Portrait* it is incorporated into the conversation with Father Butt, apparently on the assumption that the number of minor characters, foils for the protagonist to impress or be impressed by, ought to be kept to a concentrated minimum. Acting on this decision, Joyce reduces two Jesuits to one Jesuit (the dean of studies) and several scenes to one long typical scene which embraces his entire relationship with the Order: Stephen's role as student ("I will try to learn it"), the spiritual *versus* the worldly function of the Jesuits, the "secret subtle wisdom" of the Order in seeking to capture the youthful mind ("When may we expect to have something from you on the esthetic question?"), the skill in debating, within fixed limits, which the Jesuits had taught him and which he turns to account against his preceptors, his identification of the Order with the national enemy, with repression, and, as the dean sets up the career of Simon Moonan as worthy of emulation, with perversion of true spiritual values.

In order to accomplish all this in a few pages, it is necessary that the author cease to write, as he does in *Stephen Hero*, about two distinct persons whom he had met in his Jesuit college. What he says in *A Portrait* about the dean of studies must be capable of indefinite extension beyond the character itself – must be, in short, symbolic of the whole Jesuit system. In this rare instance, therefore, hundreds of words of descriptive commentary are lavished upon a character in the later book which are understandably lacking in the earlier version, where the author can sufficiently individualize his minor personalities with a recurrent word or gesture. The dean is endowed with shadowy outlines at the very start of the episode in *A Portrait*: "A figure was crouching before the large grate and by its leanness and greyness he knew that it was the dean of studies lighting the fire" (P 215). When it is remembered that the same passage in *Stephen Hero* said simply that Stephen "discovered Father Butt kneeling on the hearth-stone engaged in lighting a small fire" (S 28), the basic difference in approach will be evident. With this flat and matter-of-fact introduction of the dean in the earlier book, all Joyce can do is to bring the scene to a hurried and unambiguous conclusion in a few lines. But in *A Portrait*, the way having been prepared for imaginative elaboration by the hazy view afforded of the old teacher, the author is able to give deeper meaning to scene and man through use of the associative technique that William York Tindall describes at length in *The Literary Symbol*.[9]

As Stephen observes the dean in the dark lecture hall, the venerable figure seems to him "more than ever a humble server making ready the place of sacrifice in an empty temple, a levite of the Lord" (P 215). That Stephen is to be that burnt offering does not occur to the boy, apparently, at that moment, but to the reader the association is strong and the passage proportionally much more effective than its meager counterpart in the earlier version. With the continuing description, omitted entirely from *Stephen Hero*, it becomes obvious that the dean is representative of the Jesuits as an order. "In tending the fire upon the altar, in bearing tidings secretly, in waiting upon worldlings, in striking swiftly when bidden," in all these stereotyped pursuits Joyce characterizes not merely the role of one dean of studies but of the imposing organization which commissions him as its agent. Later in the same passage, the gray figure passes from its role as generalized Jesuit to take on the outlines of the fabled founder of the Order. "Like Ignatius he was lame but in his eyes burned no spark of Ignatius' enthusiasm." What Joyce had tried to show in *Stephen Hero*, in essay fashion, about the paralysis of the spiritual life is here symbolically rendered in the dramatic presentation of the dean of studies as lame. And while he is able to kindle a fire in the hearth, the secret springs of inspiration of the Jesuits "had not fired his soul with the energy of apostleship" (P 217). He performs his spiritual function "without joy . . . [but] with a firm gesture of obedience." Overwhelmed by his sudden intuitive knowledge of the emptiness of such a spiritual life, Stephen feels "a desolating pity," very rare in the earlier book, "for this faithful servingman of the knightly Loyola . . . one whom he would never call his ghostly father" (P 222). The climax of personal involvement has been reached. Father Butt and Stephen Daedalus making small talk in *Stephen Hero* have given way to a new pair, of formidable dimensions. Stephen's

H

necessary rejection of God and religion and father is, in this episode of *A Portrait*, the direct result of the manufactured details embroidered on the uncomplicated anecdote that Byrne recounted to his friend. And the apparently random thread of the dialogue is seen, at the climactic point, not to have been random at all. The slowness of the dean to catch the distinctions involved in Stephen's use of words is further reiteration of the inability of the clergy to speak the protagonist's language. The sensitiveness with which the young man recognizes that even his very language is, as he thinks, foreign, stresses, at the appropriate moment, his total lack of a satisfactory father image – either in fatherland or father confessor. It is at this point that the Jesuit, speaking with the authority and the wisdom of the world, holds his classmate Moonan up to him as a model for emulation in the same way that Shaun the Philistine was always placed before Shem the rebel as exemplifier of the worldly virtues. Such moral obtuseness on the part of his spiritual and educational guidance counselor is the note on which the author chooses to end the fire-lighting scene.

If Philip Handler had not already treated so thoroughly the other parallel scenes from the two versions of *A Portrait* – Stephen's relationship with his girl friend, the petition for universal peace, rowdy assaults on Stephen's integrity by boorish students – they could profitably have been studied at this point. His exhaustive study makes further comment on parallels and deviations unnecessary. Yet in other connections, the work of sifting the adolescent version of Stephen's portrait for clues to its author's habits of composition goes on. The more mature Joyce may have considered it "rubbish," but junk heaps often offer rich rewards in salvage operations. The role of Simon Dedalus in this book and the others, with special emphasis on the simoniacal implications of the name itself, for instance, has been investigated by Julian B. Kaye. The number of studies devoted to *Stephen Hero*, in spite of the massive scholarly output relating to Joyce and his

works, is insignificant. What deters critics from attempting
more than primitive, fragmentary analyses of the book is
probably its incomplete state. Such comprehensive views as
Brewster Ghiselin's of "The Unity of Joyce's 'Dubliners' "
are not likely to be taken of a manuscript which is only one-
fifth complete in its published form.[10] As the principal gloss
on many analogies which later become crucial – Stephen as
Satan, Stephen as Jesus, Stephen and Cranly in more flesh-
and-blood relationship – the early version of *A Portrait* holds
riches not yet tapped.

V | *The Early Work in Perspective*

Because Joyce's published work has an organic design, no part of it may be omitted from consideration by the critic who does not want to distort Joyce's purpose. The patently symbolic situations of his early books return to confront the reader again and again in the later ones. Though time and maturity often alter the emphasis of the symbols or the key in which they are presented, no clear dividing line can be drawn between the significance of the symbol in one book and in the next. In addition, Joyce's later works teem with echoes and overtones, faint hints, suggestions, insinuations, iterated, reinforced, and reiterated, of the work of the apprenticeship period. Just as the Sirens episode of *Ulysses* is designed to sound like a fugue, in which variations on a musical motif are played and replayed, so Joyce's entire literary canon is a controlled composition. The song "Martha" that runs through that episode is paralleled in the book as a whole by the frequent mention of Bloom's potato – one of the strands that bind together the multi-leveled intricacies of *Ulysses*. One cannot speak of finishing *Chamber Music*, or of getting to the end of *A Portrait*, or of completing *Ulysses*, for each is only a part of the book of Joyce, the last word of which the author felt he had not said even in *Finnegans Wake*.

An almost unfailing mark of the great literary artist is his ability to carry each stage of his work to its highest possible peak of development, to the point at which nothing more can fruitfully be done with the form, and then to move on to a new stage. Lesser artists seek a single formula for success and, finding it, busy themselves with turning out a profusion of works based on the initial success. Arnold Bennett, with his interminable array of large, solid, realistic novels, is a good example. Artists of the stamp of Yeats and Eliot – and Joyce – are not satisfied to remain bound by the limitations of the first form that proves workable. The early realistic verses of Eliot, in the manner of Laforgue, give way to religious poetry by direct statement in the *Four Quartets* and *The Cocktail Party*. Each stage, for men like these, is self-contained and technically as perfect as the artist can make it, but, at the same time, a relationship exists among the various stages. If there had been no first stage, certainly the succeeding stages would have been very different – or perhaps there would have been no subsequent products at all.

This is as true of Joyce as of other artists; perhaps truer, for in each of his few works can be observed, with the acuity of hindsight at least, the common thread that binds them all into an uncommon unity. It seems a far cry from the brilliant stories of *Dubliners* to the elaborate "monomyth" of H.C.E. Yet, from first to last, no matter what his medium, Joyce constantly strikes recurring notes.

Such intermingling of identical characters, pervasive themes, and stylistic devices in Joyce's work is by now recognized as a critical commonplace. What remains to be demonstrated, in specific detail, is the precise nature of the change which a motif, a structural nuance, or a character may have undergone in Joyce's literary progression. "Eveline" will suit my purpose admirably here. It is never mentioned as one of Joyce's triumphs: many critics, indeed, prefer to forget the early stories altogether as embarrassingly juvenile. It was written very early, and, the shortest story in *Dubliners*, it required only a fraction of the space of one page in *The Irish Homestead* when it appeared on September 10, 1904. If this tiny bit of Dublin life captured in prose can be shown to contain the distinctive essentials of its author's mature writing, and yet differ significantly in presentation, the demonstration may prove enlightening.

The theme of "Eveline" – escape – is a favorite of both George Moore and Joyce. For a person who felt strongly the decay of Dublin early in the century several roads lay open. He might fight back violently in the arena, using the weapons of the mob – political intrigue and bombs. Or, seeking to recall Ireland to its ancient greatness, freshness, and life by reintroducing what had been worth while in the past at the same time as he destroyed what was odious in the present, he might join the Gaelic revival movement. Or, feeling the hopelessness of an attack from within on what seemed an already dead body, he might attempt to escape contamination by putting as much distance as possible between Ireland and himself. The merits of both courses can be determined only relatively, for their effectiveness depends on the personalities who adopt them. Douglas Hyde, for instance, and Padraic Pearse, labored strenuously within Ireland and, though in very different ways, succeeded admirably. To Joyce's temperament, no such course of immediate action could appeal.

Many harsh words have been written, by those who did not

have to make the choice, concerning Joyce's "flight" from the scenes and problems of his native land. D. S. Mirsky, the Marxist literary spokesman, complains that Joyce is "an apostate-emigrant. He has run away from the reality which produced his material."[1] Mirsky blames Joyce for taking flight when he was "unable to endure the musty provincialism of the bourgeoisie of Ireland . . ."[2] From within Ireland, too, has come a stream of criticism directed against its foremost publicizer, writing off Joyce as a man of some flashy talent, who was too callous or too cowardly to assist actively in the Irish Renaissance. In *Exiles,* Joyce shows how impossible it is for an expatriate like Richard Rowan, a projection of Joyce himself, to resume a literary life in Dublin. But it may not be impertinent to suggest that, in the long view, Joyce has done more to revive respect for Ireland among thinking people, more to bring before a world-wide audience dramatically and sharply the problems of twentieth-century Ireland, than perhaps any of her splendid-hearted but short-lived patriots and her demanding journalist-critics.

That, however, is not the main point. What matters is Joyce's knowledge of his own powers, his early decision that only away from Ireland could he "forge . . . the uncreated conscience" of his race. He was willing to bear the scorn of Shaun-like citizens who deemed him a deserter, in order to create literature in freedom.[3] There is no doubt, either, that Joyce was bothered during his adolescence and young manhood by this problem of escape, which seemed central to him for all serious-minded Irishmen. A good indication of how important he thought it is the number of times it appears as a main or subsidiary theme in *Dubliners* and in his later books. It is unnecessary to touch again upon the way in which escape fills the minds of the boys in "An Encounter," or how "Araby" conjures up visions of a better place than Dublin to an impressionable adolescent, or with what pain Little Chandler tests the walls of his cage.

Using the now familiar flash-back technique, unusual in

1900, Joyce tells the story of Eveline, the accustomed tale of hardship and poverty unrelieved almost by any beauty in the life of a lower-middle-class Irish family. The daughter, just out of her teens, gazes out at the drab Dublin street, thinking of her unpleasant life as foster mother, since their mother's death, of her younger brothers and sisters; of her job as a much abused saleslady in a Dublin department store; of her deteriorating relationship with her violent and often drunken father, who allows her almost no freedom. Her immediate problem is whether or not to escape by emigration from this sordidness, as so many of her countrymen have been doing, especially since the time of The Famine. The way lies open for the taking: her sailor friend Frank wants to carry her off as his wife to "Buenos Ayres" and freedom. She is tempted to break the ties which bind her to ways she has always thought she hated, but when the moment comes to make the irrevocable choice, she hesitates. The few bright spots in her former existence seem brighter in the light of anticipated deprivation. The chains of convention, habit, and a vow to her dying mother are too strong. She is unable to open the door of her prison, and she rejects escape "like a helpless animal" (D 48), rooted to the soil, unable to move.

Joyce does not imply any condemnation of Eveline for not doing as he himself had done. Nor, in any of the "escape" stories, is the main character able to bring himself to the point of throwing off his national shackles. The author is dealing with "little" people, it must be remembered, and, as a realist, is telling the truth. His characters do what most Dubliners do: they have occasional glimpses of a life beyond their own, but most never penetrate through the daydream stage, living and dying in the narrow confines of their "priest-ridden" and faction-torn metropolis. Foreign influences are attractive just so long as they remain foreign.

Eveline is roused from her accustomed lethargy and feels herself closest to happiness and exhilaration at those moments when she is allowed to forget her life in Dublin. These glances at freedom beyond, though infrequent, make the deepest impression upon her. Her mind turns often, during her childhood, to the priest, now an emigrant to Melbourne – and a representation of escape – whose photograph her father still keeps on the wall. She is thrilled even more by her fiancé, Frank the sailor, whose costume and appearance breathe adventure in foreign lands. His talk is of "distant countries" and "the terrible Patagonians." The romantic scenes and the very name of Balfe's operetta, *The Bohemian Girl*, make her feel elated. Even her father, whom she has little reason to love, remains most pleasantly in her memory for his unusual thoughtfulness on the day that "he had read her out a ghost story," a romantic means of escape from her life. Conversely, she cannot forgive him for sending away from the window an organ-player who played outside her mother's sickroom a "melancholy air of Italy."

The thought of her mother, whom Dublin has driven mad, as it has Father Flynn of "The Sisters," puts her in panic. "Escape! She must escape! Frank would save her." But Eveline does not realize that it is too late; she has been so long a prisoner in her mind that, like long-term convicts who are suddenly released, she cannot tolerate freedom. Prison imagery dominates the end of the story. At the dock, she "gripped with both hands at the iron railing" which leads up the gangplank. "No! No! No! It was impossible." There is a barrier beyond which this Dubliner cannot go. Frank "rushed beyond the barrier," leaving her behind, trapped by her mind and her environment. Dublin has won. Given a chance of life, Eveline has chosen symbolic death. She has refused to set forth over the water (D 48).

The early (*Irish Homestead*) version of "Eveline" [4] is substantially the same as the final treatment. Unlike the extensive revision in "The Sisters," changes in this story are limited to altered paragraphing, elimination of clumsy phrases or substitution of simple idioms for occasionally long-winded diction. Thus, for instance, "passing in review all its familiar objects" becomes "reviewing all its familiar objects." Occasionally too, in the later version explicit introductions give way to unheralded quotations of dialogue. Notice this from the *Irish Homestead* draft:

> Miss Gavan would probably be glad. She, too, would not be sorry to be out of Miss Gavan's clutches. Miss Gavan had an "edge" on her, and used her superior position mercilessly, particularly whenever there were people listening. It was – "Miss Hill, will you please attend to these ladies?" "A little bit smarter, Miss Hill, if you please." [5]

And this simpler, less obviously dramatic version from *Dubliners*:

> Miss Gavan would be glad. She had always had an edge on her, especially whenever there were people listening.
> "Miss Hill, don't you see these ladies are waiting?"
> "Look lively, Miss Hill, please." (D 43-44)

Both versions have the same abundant imagery of escape from routine, and of the ugliness which leads Eveline's mother, and may one day lead Eveline herself, to "final craziness." Father Flynn's mind breaks down too, and Mr. Breen's in *Ulysses*. Dublin life is too much for them.

First of all, Joyce must motivate the pressing need for escape; so as his symbol of the young girl's present life he selects "dust," with its associative overtones of death, disintegration, filth, and drabness. This dust is not merely without; it has worked itself into her very system, weakening her will to ameliorate her condition, wearing down the sharpness of her mind until it becomes almost animal-like in its panic at the thought of a new habitat. When this occurs, living has become simply a matter of routine surrender to an unwholesome environment and of satisfaction of bodily needs. "Her head was leaned against the window curtains and in her nostrils was the odour of dusty cretonne. She was tired" (D 42). Reinforcing his symbol wherever he can, Joyce soon adds that "she had dusted once a week for so many years, wondering where on earth all the dust came from" (D 43). Her

room, her belongings, her city, are all permeated by the re-
lentless particles. They appear to act as a drug upon her
powers of motion, for "her time was running out but she
continued to sit by the window, leaning her head against
the window curtain, inhaling the odour of dusty cretonne"
(D 46–47). Eveline is so far gone that, ironically, she prefers
at the last moment to return to dust (symbolic death?) rather
than to risk rejecting her paralyzed state by setting forth to a
new life.

The vacillating heroine of "Eveline" appears to be an early
sketch of a character who bears a different name in *Ulysses*.
The partially autobiographical Stephen Dedalus is seldom a
sympathetic figure in that book. One of the few instances in
which he redeems himself as a very human being is his meeting with his sister Dilly in the Wandering Rocks episode
(U 239–240). The young girl appears briefly here, is seen
through the eyes of her coldly intellectual brother, and disappears into the Dublin environment. In the brief moment
of her presence, however, she seems to be a reincarnation
of Eveline, this time seen from a distance, through the
detached though intensely concerned consciousness of her
brother. A comparison of the two girls may demonstrate
Joyce's advance in artistry from the early book to the later.

In "Eveline," the weak protagonist is examined mainly
from within. Even the paragraphs of ostensible description
are given in the rhythms of Eveline's circuitous thought patterns and in the querulous accents of her speech:

> One time there used to be a field there in which they used to
> play every evening with other people's children. Then a man
> from Belfast bought the field and built houses in it – not like
> their little brown houses but bright brick houses with shining
> roofs. The children of the avenue used to play together in that
> field. (D 42)

The point of view throughout is Eveline's and the method a
modification of the stream of consciousness. In that such
limitation of focus is a challenge to the author (as Henry

James's presentation of a sophisticated narrative through the consciousness of young Maisie was), Joyce as literary novice here shows remarkable control in handling a difficult, self-imposed assignment. His early choice of method, however, precludes the objectivity of distance and substitutes pathos for tragedy.

Ulysses offers two snippets of Dilly's life in Dublin, both in the episode of the Wandering Rocks. The first, without benefit of the formal paraphernalia for indicating a stage play (i.e., the names of the speakers preceding the words of dialogue, stage directions in italics or parentheses), is nothing more than such a dramatic version (U 233–235). Omniscient and reportorially neutral, the author records the conversation of Dilly and her father without comment, allowing the reader to supply his own indictment of the relationship. The second short scene involving Dilly – a brief twenty-eight lines – is reported from the point of view of Stephen Dedalus and rises, in its climactic lyricism, to tragic intensity. As one reads these two scenes, the conclusion that Dilly is a sketch of Eveline becomes increasingly clear.

The relationship of father to child is identical. Simon Dedalus immediately seeks to overawe and master his now motherless daughter. "– Stand up straight for the love of the Lord Jesus, Mr. Dedalus said. Are you trying to imitate your uncle John? . . ." (U 234.) But Eveline, in spite of feeling "herself in danger of her father's violence," plucks up courage once each week when money is needed to feed the family.

> Besides, the invariable squabble for money on Saturday nights had begun to weary her unspeakably. She always gave her entire wages . . . . but the trouble was to get any money from her father. He said she used to squander the money . . . that he wasn't going to give her his hard-earned money to throw about the streets . . . . In the end he would give her the money and ask her had she any intention of buying Sunday's dinner . . . . (D 44)

Similarly, in answer to Dilly's insistent request for the family allowance, Mr. Dedalus seeks to evade compliance. His "Where would I get the money?" turns, at Dilly's persistence, to drunken menace:

> – Wait awhile, Mr Dedalus said threateningly. You're like the rest of them, are you? An insolent pack of little bitches since your poor mother died. But wait awhile. You'll all get a short shrift and a long day from me. Low blackguardism! I'm going to get rid of you. Wouldn't care if I was stretched out stiff . . . . (U 234)

Eveline's admission that her father had "latterly . . . begun to threaten her and say what he would do to her only for her dead mother's sake" is certainly re-echoed in this passage from *Ulysses*. Furthermore, Mr. Dedalus, like his earlier prototype in "Eveline," does indeed end by reluctantly surrendering the necessary money. The ironically neutral tone with which this entire episode is recorded by Joyce creates an effect immeasurably more potent and poignant than the too personal, too restricted view in the *Dubliners* story.

The Stephen-Dilly meeting in the Wandering Rocks chapter acts, it seems to me, as corroboration that Joyce intended the girl to be an extension of the heroine of "Eveline." Stephen and his sister meet accidentally at a book cart, where both, unused to real social or intellectual rapport, fumble for words. Dilly is thrilled but embarrassed to confess that she has just bought a secondhand French primer. Equally moved by this unexpected view of his sister as something other than a weak, colorless household drudge, Stephen is sophisticated enough to hide his thoughts. That Dilly should covet culture for its intellectual satisfactions is less likely than that the French primer represents to her the kind of escape which *The Bohemian Girl* or Melbourne or "Buenos Ayres" offers to Eveline. The significant figure of speech common to the short story and to this episode of the novel appears at the climactic moment of both. As the sailor Frank tries to lead Eveline up the gangway of the ship to freedom, the paralyzing effect of Dublin is too strong. "All the seas of the

world tumbled about her heart. He was drawing her into
them: he would drown her. She gripped with both hands at
the iron railing" (D 48). By not leaving, by refusing to set out
on the freedom-giving water, Eveline chooses death in dear,
dusty Dublin. Joyce extends and alters the image in *Ulysses*,
but retains the idea of death by drowning:

> She is drowning. Agenbite. Save her. Agenbite. All against
> us. She will drown me with her, eyes and hair. Lank coils of
> seaweed hair around me, my heart, my soul. Salt green death.
> (U 240)

There is no comparison, of course – and that is why I have
belabored the Eveline-Dilly relationship perhaps at too great
length – between the poverty of associative context for the
climactic figure in the short story and the richness of texture
in the later novel. That *Ulysses* is a long book and "Eveline"
is the shortest story in *Dubliners* has much to do with this
result. Yet, without trying to dictate to Joyce what he might
have done, a reader may suggest that the author's substitution, almost arbitrarily, of death in a watery grave for the
more appropriate snuffing out in a handful of dust seems an
unnecessary waste of a carefully built-up symbol. In *Ulysses*,
quite to the contrary, the "salt green death" has been fore-
shadowed by the salt of their mother's tears, by the green of
her vomitings, by the drowned man in the Proteus episode,
by the national color of Ireland, and, finally, by association
with Homeric panoramas.

To the critic interested in Joyce's early prose as harboring
in embryo the seeds of his later stylistic devices, "Eveline"
amply repays analysis in the same way as the changing prose
style of *A Portrait* does. Joyce apparently wishes to give the
impression that Eveline is a dull, slow-witted girl, able to
think only in a most pedestrian way about the most element-
ary subjects, never on an abstract level. Nowhere does the
author say this, but the tenor of his prose, as he describes her
thought process, seems unmistakable. The sentences are
monotonous in their sameness, all of the subject-verb-object

type. Lack of subordination makes for a jaggedness and a deliberate simplicity of movement which Joyce reserves for depiction of childhood or dull maturity. A long paragraph will serve as sufficient example:

> Few people passed. The man out of the last house passed on his way home; she heard his footsteps clacking along the concrete pavement and afterwards crunching on the cinder path before the new red houses. One time there used to be a field there in which they used to play every evening with other people's children. Then a man from Belfast bought the field and built houses in it – not like their little brown houses but bright brick houses with shining roofs. The children of the avenue used to play together in that field – the Devines, the Waters, the Dunns, little Keogh the cripple, she and her brothers and sisters. Ernest, however, never played: he was too grown up. Her father used often to hunt them in out of the field with his blackthorn stick; but usually little Keogh used to keep *nix* and call out when he saw her father coming. Still they seemed to have been rather happy then. Her father was not so bad then; and besides, her mother was alive. That was a long time ago; she and her brothers and sisters were all grown up; her mother was dead. Tizzie Dunn was dead, too, and the Waters had gone back to England. Everything changes. Now she was going to go away like the others, to leave her home.
> (D 42)

The sense, the sound, the rhythms of insinuating sameness support the reader's impression of overwhelming naïveté, and perhaps more than that, stupidity. But probably the most effective stylistic device in the paragraph, and in the story, is Joyce's insistent repetition of key words to convey the movement of a slow mind which plays with important nouns and verbs, much as little children do when they are learning to speak. Thus, she thinks of the "new red houses," and the man from Belfast who "built houses," "not like their little brown houses but bright brick houses." Certainly Joyce was skillful enough to have avoided this excessive repetition had he not wished to make the prose almost unbearably slow-moving at this point. The same device can be seen at work in other instances in this passage. It may be, of course, that the circular movement of the prose is meant to convey more a sense of tiredness and lassitude than of unintelligence, for Joyce tells the reader that Eveline "was tired," but her subsequent thoughts and actions do not argue a quick mind.

Though known for the lavish abundance of his stylistic devices, Joyce seldom discarded a technique once it had worked well for him. It is not surprising, therefore, that the "tired" prose of "Eveline" should turn up twenty years later as the central method of the fifty-three-page Eumaeus episode of *Ulysses* (U 596–649). Joyce has by this time extended it so that the effect is attained by more than the repetition of important words and ideas. Now sentences trail off into nothingness, grammatical constructions are mixed, subordination is logically reversed, tenses lose their normal sequence – all to indicate the mental and physical weariness of the actors in the drama, at one o'clock in the morning, after they have left the brothel of Bella Cohen. A typical paragraph shows the method:

> The spirit moving him, he would much have liked to follow Jack Tar's good example and leave the likeness there for a very few minutes to speak for itself on the plea he . . . [all ellipsis marks in this paragraph are Joyce's] so that the other could drink in the beauty for himself, her stage presence being, frankly, a treat in itself which the camera could not at all do justice to. But it was scarcely professional etiquette so, though it was a warm pleasant sort of a night now yet wonderfully cool for the season considering, for sunshine after storm . . . . And he did feel a kind of need there and then to follow suit like a kind of inward voice and satisfy a possible need by moving a motion. Nevertheless, he sat tight, just viewing the slightly soiled photo creased by opulent curves, none the worse for wear, however, and looked away thoughtfully with the intention of not further increasing the other's possible embarrassment while gauging her symmetry of heaving *embonpoint.* (U 637)

The paragraph continues beyond this point, but there is no need to quote further. The clichés that flow easily from tired minds, the interminably rambling sentences, the absence of crisp thought all operate to build up the impression Joyce wants to create.

There is a school of thought that approves of the limited use to which Joyce puts his style of calculated rhythmical mimicry, on a small scale, in the short story, but objects to extended dependence on the same principle in half a hundred pages of the novel. If Joyce wishes to induce in his readers through the vagaries of prose style the same degree of weariness from which his fictional characters suffer, he must run the risk that the readers will indeed succumb, as Bloom does, to the insidious chanting of "Sinbad the Sailor and Tinbad the Tailor and Jinbad the Jailor and Whinbad the Whaler. . . ." It is quite possible to carry imitation of the banal and the dull to a point beyond which the audience, ceasing to appreciate intellectually the performance of the stylist, surrenders to literary suggestion and drowses over the dullness. Joyce almost compulsively refused to allow the possibility for his ideal reader. From the short stories to the novel of adolescence, through *Ulysses* to *Finnegans Wake*, he felt it essential to increase the dosage – to go beyond the boundaries his earlier efforts had erected. The faint outlines of the technique in "Eveline" become the stylistic excess of Bloomsday and show clearly the way he had to travel.

Another early story which is excellently illustrative of the road which Joyce's genius took from apprenticeship to maturity is "Grace." Though it is one of his best, and, after "The Dead," his longest and most ambitious, I have been unable to find even one serious critical treatment of its art.[6] Except for brief and uninformative notice in a few places, critics have ignored its considerable importance as a preparation for the technical problems which Joyce would face in *Ulysses*.

In "Grace" (1905) Joyce first experiments seriously with gentle juxtaposition of a public and universal mythical structure, on the one hand, and, on the other, a sordid contemporary narrative. It stands to reason that *Ulysses*, his notorious

I

culmination of such an effort, did not spring full-grown from the mature talent of its literary father. "Grace" allowed Joyce to test his skill at simultaneous presentation of two cultures, two ways of thought, two views of, say, grace, religious ecstasy, and the fullness of human life. That he decided in the later book to make the comparison explicit by calling the effort *Ulysses* is probably explicable in terms of the lack of discernment with which the public had greeted his earlier employment of the technique in the short story.

Joyce superimposes upon the unlovely vista of modern religious life in Ireland the rich associative values of the Renaissance in "Grace," by employing what Stanislaus Joyce calls "an obvious touch of parody on *The Divine Comedy*." [7] Deliberately, he sacrifices his own flair for colorful display in order that, by contrast with the weak and degraded picture of modern Hell which he draws, Dante's magnificent conception may appear even more gorgeous. By association, the firm and beautiful Catholic religious structure of the past may put to shame the pallid shell of orthodoxy that, in Joyce's opinion, passed for true belief in the Dublin of 1900.

It was not necessary for Joyce to follow out in detail the complicated plot and symbolic structure of Dante's poem. Nor would such a procedure have made a better story for the Irishman. He had only to suggest in broad outline a similarity between the two works. This he does, first, by making a threefold division in the story (as he does later in *Ulysses*), the parts representing Inferno, Purgatorio, and Paradiso. Appropriately, the realist in Joyce causes him to select the dirty floor of a lavatory in a pub as his symbol of the wretchedness of Hell. The first paragraph of the story, as usual, fills in important details of the motif of the descent to the infernal regions:

> Two gentlemen who were in the lavatory at the time tried to lift him up: but he was quite helpless. He lay curled up at the foot of the stairs down which he had fallen. They succeeded in turning him over. His hat had rolled a few yards away and his

clothes were smeared with the filth and ooze of the floor on which he had lain, face downwards. His eyes were closed and he breathed with a grunting noise. A thin stream of blood trickled from the corner of his mouth. (D 190)

The reader will notice that Mr. Kernan's descent has been headlong down the stairs, and that symbolically, as well as actually, he cannot be lifted up. Complete helplessness, characteristic of so many Dubliners, marks his condition, for he has fallen from grace. Dazed and confused, like Satan and his cohorts on Milton's burning lake, he is begrimed by the filth of the world. He is too confounded to worry even about his hat, representative to him of social prestige and gentility. More an animal than a man in his degraded state, he makes grunting noises and he cannot see, lying eyes closed and face downward.

His companions in dissipation have deserted him; his identity is unknown. In the bar, his reclining form is surrounded by a crowd of unsympathetic, gawking onlookers, until officialdom takes a hand in the person of an "immense constable." He is not particularly interested in the body or the soul of Mr. Kernan, but simply in the routine duty of recording the circumstances of the fall and assigning responsibility. It takes an outsider, neither a patron of the bar nor an alleged friend of the victim, to play the part of the Good Samaritan. As ambiguous as the misty figure who rides in and out of the picture in the eighteenth passus of *The Vision of Piers Plowman*, or the dour Macintosh in *Ulysses*, this young man "in a cycling-suit" immediately takes command of the situation to rescue Kernan from the Hell in which he finds him. His actions are decidedly consistent with Christian religious symbolism. "He knelt down promptly beside the injured man and called for water," seeking, it would seem, to relieve bodily pain but also to purify spiritually. His motions recall the administration of a sacrament. Typically, the cyclist takes "the man by the . . . arm" to lead him away from the place of his sins, refusing as he does so to accept the thanks of the grateful sufferer. He passes from the story as swiftly as he enters it, his name unknown and his function left to speculation. Only one more reference is made to him in a later conversation, when he is called "a decent young chap, that medical fellow." So the reader learns that the shadowy figure is a healer. Perhaps the very ambiguity which allows one to attribute to him the qualities of Good Samaritan, Christ, good angel, and the rest, makes his simple act all the more impressive. Compared to the very unambiguous and unsubtle type of Christian doctrine preached later by the easily identifiable Father Purdon, the actions of the unknown man are exemplary. His selfless act reminds one of Bloom's rescue of Stephen in the Circe chapter.

The first of the three parts of the story ends with Kernan restored to his family, but still apparently not restored to grace, for the sinner has not repented nor given evidence that he is ready to "wash the pot." In the final line of the section his friend Mr. Power assures Kernan's wife that "We'll make a new man of him" (D 197). The way in which Mr. Kernan is prepared by his friends to enter heaven is left to the second, or Purgatorio, section of "Grace."

Here, what has been almost a parable in Part I receives explicit commentary; in this section Joyce comes out from behind a veil of parody and symbolism to report coldly and disgustedly on the state of current religious ecstasy in Dublin. The way the winds of religion are blowing is clear in the fact that it requires an elaborate trick on the part of Kernan's friends, Martin Cunningham, Power, and M'Coy, to get Kernan to agree to enter the blessed state in which the sinner may have grace offered to him. Appeal must be made to social prestige, self-interest, personal vanity, before the religious ritual will be embraced. It is not so much that Kernan wishes to attend a church service as that he is unwilling to be left out of anything in which his friends are active. For the Philistines of Dublin, salesmen and constabulary officials like Kernan and Power, religion has become not a matter of heart

and spirit but of practical considerations, good business, a sop
to conscience, and a prop of respectability – in much the
same way that Kernan's silk hat is all these things.

Practicality is the keynote of the story. Mrs. Kernan is an
"active, practical woman" who measures the goodness of her
two sons by the number of letters she receives from them and
by their practice of sometimes sending home "money."
"Religion for her was a habit," as it was for so many Dubliners, and though she is sensible enough to hold out little hope
for her husband's conversion to the paths of righteousness,
she is flattered by "influential" Mr. Cunningham's willingness to try. He too, in *Ulysses*, is a "good practical catholic."
". . . Religion was religion. The scheme might do good and,
at least, it could do no harm" (D 200). In this negative way,
almost all the actions in "Grace" are undertaken. When the
scheme of making a retreat is mentioned to Kernan, it is
cloaked in flippant slang, for the practical men of affairs are
bashful and inarticulate when they try to discuss their spiritual shortcomings. "So we're going to wash the pot together."
And later, "D'ye know what, Tom, has just occurred to me?
You might join in and we'd have a four-handed reel." Perhaps the best example of practical judgment in religious
affairs is given when Mr. M'Coy, seconding Cunningham's
opinion that the Jesuits are the "grandest order in the
Church," agrees because "if you want a thing well done and
no flies about, you go to a Jesuit. They're the boyos have
influence . . . ." (D 208)

The lost soul, Kernan, considers in silence the invitation to
join the retreat. He is not overcome with awe or remorse. The
silence proceeds from his wish to "show a stiff neck" at such
a time. He is impressed by the knowledge that the retreat is
exclusively for businessmen, and that the priest in charge of
it has a reputation for being lenient with sinners. Nervously
yet belligerently he faces the ordeal, but he draws the line at
several details of the ancient ritual. The diction that Joyce
uses at this point is obvious and appropriate, for it strips away

any spiritual pretensions that may have surrounded the daily rituals of the church. (The key words are not italicized in Joyce's text:)

> ". . . Must I have a candle?"
> "O yes," said Mr. Cunningham.
> "No, *damn* it all," said Mr. Kernan *sensibly*, "I draw the line there. I'll do the *job* right enough. I'll do the *retreat business* and confession, and . . . all that *business*. But . . . no candles! No, *damn* it all, I bar the candles!"
>
> . . . .
> "I bar the *magic-lantern business*."
> "Everyone laughed heartily." (D 218–219)

At this point the second section ends. There is no need to mention how ill-prepared these typical members of the lower middle class are to enter the Paradiso which should be their next step, when their period in purgatory is completed. Kernan's refusal to accept the light (candle) is symbolic. The conversation of the second part reveals them a prey to most of the sins which beset fallen man. If they are admitted to heavenly grace, it must be to a very limited one, a heaven suited to their spiritual attitudes.

Ironically maybe, Joyce selects the transept of "the Jesuit Church in Gardiner Street" as the locale of Kernan's heaven. It is a distinctively bourgeois heaven peopled by "gentlemen" who are "well dressed and orderly." Among the respectable churchgoers present, Joyce is quick to point out "Mr. Harford, the moneylender," Mr. Fanning, the "mayor maker" and sinister campaign treasurer of "Ivy Day in the Committee Room," and Michael Grimes, "the owner of three pawnbroker's shops." It is a usurer's heaven (D 220).

The people in the pews seem much more interested in the care of their bodies and of their material possessions than of their souls. Kernan's hat, "rehabilitated by his wife," once more exudes respectability as it rests firmly in his lap. When the ceremony calls for the congregation to go down on its knees, all "produced handkerchiefs and knelt upon them with care." Father Purdon too pays careful attention to the folds of the wide sleeve of his surplice. His sermon, ignoring the unambiguous statement in Matthew that "Ye cannot serve God and Mammon," seems intent upon cajoling the practical, well-to-do audience into blissful spiritual security by the in-sinuating smoothness of a Belial. Speaking to them as a "man of the world," Purdon uses the diction of the businessman, the metaphor of the "spiritual accountant," which so sickens Joyce that he will not even deign to comment upon it. He simply allows the sermon to condemn the one who delivers it. The author finds revolting the wishy-washy attitude of con-doning sins committed in the practical life of the world, so long as the sinner hypocritically can say: "Well, I have look-ed into my accounts. I find this wrong and this wrong. But, with God's grace, I will rectify this and this. I will set right my accounts" (D 223).

The Joyce-writes-whatever-comes-into-his-head school of criticism frequently adduces evidence for its point of view from such stories as "Ivy Day in the Committtee Room" and "Grace." The long and apparently rambling conversations, the seemingly plotless narrative, and the inconclusively ex-pressed endings offer superficial support. But just as careful study of *Ulysses*, with the aid of Hanley's *Word Index*,[8] turns up innumerable parallel and symmetrical strands – one motif almost mathematically placed with respect to the next, in well planned profusion – so "Grace," for instance, even in its expansive reaches, demonstrates Joyce's calculated regard for symmetry. The three-part Dantean structure has been examined. But within that structure, it can be shown that concern for form extends to the minutiae of composition.

Throughout the story, for example, Joyce seems to be drawing a parallel between the Dublin police force and the Dublin priesthood. The one group is responsible for law and order in the physical sense – governing the body – while the other has the responsibility of keeping the spirit safe and secure. The clergy, Joyce seems to feel, are no more delicate and sensitive in the administering of their trust than the constabulary of theirs. The crowded pub is paralleled by the crowded church. The silk hat is dirty and disordered in the Hell of the pub lavatory, but the respectability of the businessman's heaven is evidenced by the restoration of the hat to its normal position. The "immense constable" who enters, notebook ready, and goes stolidly and without feeling at getting the facts of the physical accident, plays the same role as Father Purdon later. The priest is also described as "massive" and is just as impersonal in his approach to this matter of routine business. "A powerful-looking figure, the upper part of which was draped with a white surplice, was observed to be struggling up into the pulpit" (D 220). Notice the impersonality of Joyce's description. Just as the constable has knelt at the prostrate body of Kernan and called for brandy to revive the physical man, the priest kneels and prays for the restoration of a prostrate soul. The constable draws off his glove and looks round at the ring of onlookers; "The preacher turned back each wide sleeve . . . and slowly surveyed the array of faces."

If these supposed similarities are coincidental and not the result of a deliberately drawn comparison and contrast, then it is difficult to explain much of the rambling conversation about policemen and priests in the expansive second section of "Grace." Mr. Kernan complains of the necessity of supporting by taxes "these ignorant bostooms" of the constabulary. In an anecdote Mr. Cunningham gives concrete example of their crudeness and lack of genteel refinement. But he has to admit that, "like everything else in this world . . . . You get some bad ones and you get some good ones" (D 205). Several minutes later, speaking of the Jesuit Order, he assigns almost the same derogatory epithets to the priests who cater to the lower classes: "It's some of those secular priests, ignorant, bumptious –" but Mr. Cunningham breaks in with a remark very similar to his statement on the police: "They're all good men . . . each in his own way" (D 208–209).[9] The repeated comparison of police and priesthood is supposed to show that both groups have allowed their functions to become flatly identical.

The policeman-priest linkage is not an artificial one, invented to supply conversational material in "Grace" alone. That Joyce has given it a great deal of thought is evident from the frequency with which it crops up in his books. He delights in coupling one group with the other. In *A Portrait*, for instance, he rails at the idol of Irish womanhood – "a priested peasant, with a brother a policeman." In the same book, also, he suggests indirectly the point of the story Cunningham tells about the eating habits of the constabulary ("65, catch your cabbage"). Speaking of the heads of the Catholic hierarchy in Ireland, Mr. Dedalus mentions scathingly "the tub of guts up in Armagh." He goes on: "He has a handsome face, mind you, in repose. You should see that fellow lapping up his . . . cabbage of a cold winter's day" (P 33). Here again, Joyce is apparently stressing the coarse earthiness of two supposedly dissimilar professions. In Dublin, Joyce says, both bodies are composed of the same kind of men, with the same type of mentality, performing very similar, non-spiritual, routine duties and both living on contributions of tax-paying and churchgoing Dubliners. In Joyce's city, hell and heaven seem equally a matter of physical comfort and mental drowsiness.

Much more than this, however, is revealed about the decay of religion, or perhaps of the religious spirit, in the long conversation in "Grace." Beneath the matter-of-fact presentation of the spoken thoughts of a handful of ordinary Dublin Catholics can be heard the mocking laughter of the author. He is witness to the muddled conglomeration of religious misstatements and distortions sincerely espoused alike by the piously and impiously ignorant. Mottoes in questionable Latin, glib clichés, take the place of real thought. Small inanities pompously uttered pass for weighty observations in the vapid atmosphere of decaying Dublin. The group in Mr.

Kernan's bedroom dismisses in one or two phrases Pope Leo XIII's aim in life, his predilection for scholarship, his "strong face," and his poetry on the invention of the photograph – "in Latin, of course." They mix up the names of the chief disputants in the papal infallibility controversy. But the height of tautological absurdity is reached in the serious, straight-faced discussion concerning *ex cathedra* pronouncements of the popes. Mr. Cunningham declares that

> ". . . not one of them ever preached *ex cathedra* a word of false doctrine. Now isn't that an astonishing thing?"
> "That is," said Mr. Kernan.
> "Yes, because when the Pope speaks *ex cathedra*," Mr. Fogarty explained, "he is infallible."
> "Yes," said Mr. Cunningham. (D 214–215)

And the argument goes round in a circle.

These Dubliners have a vague and distorted knowledge of the history of their Church. They know even less about Latin, the language of the religion. The practical Catholic, Martin Cunningham, gives the motto of Pope Leo as "Lux upon Lux, apparently ignorant of the fact that the word "upon" does not exist in Latin. Mr. Fogarty knows enough to use the word *"in"* rather than "upon," but he and M'Coy vacillate between *"Tenebris"* and *"Tenebrae"* in the motto *"Lux in Tenebris."* Considerably annoyed, Cunningham insists "positively" upon the correctness of *"Lux upon Lux."* "The inference," Joyce slyly adds, "was allowed."

While the author attests to the deterioration in the quality of response to religion, at the same time he shows that the blind faith of those subjected to the orthodox religious training of Dublin parochial schools is still powerful. When talk turns to the Protestants, M'Coy introduces points of similarity between Catholic and dissenting belief.

> "We both believe in – "
> He hesitated for a moment. [significantly]
> ". . . in the Redeemer. Only they don't believe in the Pope and in the mother of God."

"But, of course," said Mr. Cunningham quietly and effectively, "our religion is *the* religion, the old original faith."

"Not a doubt of it," said Mr. Kernan, warmly. (D 211)

Even the cynical and the indifferent will agree on vague generalities in which they have been thoroughly schooled. This holds true also in a more local sense. Not only is their religion "*the* religion," but "The Irish priesthood is honoured all the world over." And, Mr. M'Coy interjects, "Not like some of the other priesthoods on the continent . . . unworthy of the name" (D 209).

Joyce's disgust with practical religion, empty of true religious emotion, extends beyond "Grace" to *Ulysses* and the *Wake*. In the stream of Bloom's consciousness he pours out accumulated venom. Bloom, watching communion services, thinks of the mundane reasons behind supposedly sacred ritual:

> The priest bent down to put it into her mouth, murmuring all the time. Latin . . . . What? *Corpus*. Body Corpse. Good idea the Latin. Stupefies them first. (U 79)

Observing the effect of receiving the sacramental bread, he goes on:

> Look at them. Now I bet it makes them feel happy. Lollipop. It does . . . . There's a big idea behind it, kind of kingdom of God is within you feel . . . . Let off steam . . . . (U 80)

Bloom decides that it is all right for the priest not to give the communicants any of the wine from the chalice. "Doesn't give them any of it: shew wine: only the other. Cold comfort. Pious fraud but quite right: otherwise they'd have one old booser worse than another coming along, cadging for a drink" (U 80). This is surely reducing the entire ritual to unabashed pragmatic terms. Going further, Bloom lowers confession to the status of a "Great weapon in their hands." Finally, hearing the murmur of prayers in a nearby church as he sits on the darkening beach in the Nausicaa episode, Bloom approves the repetition in the replies of the congregation as sound advertising technique and nothing more.

> Mass seems to be over. Could hear them all at it. Pray for us. And pray for us. And pray for us. Good idea the repetition. Same thing with ads. Buy from us. And buy from us. (U 371)

This is the orientation toward religion possessed by the group in Kernan's bedroom.

Almost as interesting as tracing the motifs in *Dubliners* or *A Portrait* at several stages of Joyce's mental, emotional, and literary development is an examination of characters who appear in the earlier books and are introduced again in the later ones, notably in *Ulysses*. One of these, M'Coy, may well have been an early sketch of the character of Mr. Bloom, or Mr. Hunter, as the wanderer was originally supposed to have been named. As he appears in "Grace," M'Coy has the same relationship to his associates as Bloom was to have later: "His line of life had not been the shortest distance between two points and for short periods he had been driven to live by his wits. He had been . . . a canvasser for advertisements for *The Irish Times* and for *The Freeman's Journal*" (D 201). He is the submissive one in any discussion, a hanger-on, isolated from true companionship among his fellows. Mr. Power is annoyed when M'Coy has the audacity to call him by his Christian name (D 203) and ignores him as Lawyer Menton ignores Bloom's overtures of friendship in *Ulysses* (U 114). He plays up to the prejudices of his companions in order to win their good will, agreeing with Mr. Kernan that the Irish police are ignorant yahoos. "It's better to have nothing to say to them," he says with an air of finality (D 205). But even his willingness to subordinate himself to the personalities of others does not win close friendship for him; it seems rather to incline the more self-assertive members of the group simply to tolerate him. His feeling of apartness and loneliness probably reaches its height, when, in the "heaven" of the Jesuit church in Gardiner Street, he still finds himself on a bench alone, though Mr. Cunningham is paired with Mr. Kernan, and Mr. Power with Mr. Fogarty.

> Mr. M'Coy had tried unsuccessfully to find a place in the bench with the others, and, when the party had settled down in the form of a quincunx, he had tried unsuccessfully to make comic remarks. As these had not been well received, he had desisted. (D 219–220)

In these situations, if the name "Bloom" had been substituted for "M'Coy," the reader would undoubtedly have found no inconsistency in the characterization.

There is further evidence to support this view. Bloom's somewhat hazy interest in science is found also in M'Coy. The one point about which the latter is certain and on which he brooks no challenge is a scientific question:

> "No," said Mr. Kernan. "I think I caught cold on the car. There's something keeps coming into my throat, phlegm or – "
> " Mucus," said Mr. M'Coy.
> "It keeps coming like from down in my throat; sickening thing."
> "Yes, yes," said Mr. M'Coy, "that's the thorax."
> He looked at Mr. Cunningham and Mr. Power at the same time with an air of challenge. (D 201)

Furthermore, M'Coy's wife is a concert soprano, like Molly Bloom, who frequently tours the country on singing engagements. Knowing Joyce's delight in the ironic *tour de force*, the reader should not be too surprised if, in *Ulysses*, the author introduced both the early model for Bloom, and the more mature conception, Leopold Bloom – and went further, bringing them face to face at key points in the book:

> – Hello, Bloom. Where are you off to?
> – Hello, M'Coy. Nowhere in particular.
> – How's the body?
> – Fine. How are you?
> – Just keeping alive, M'Coy said. (U 72)

Interestingly too, although Bloom seems overanxious to meet and impress favorably almost all Dubliners, he draws the line at M'Coy and constantly tries to "get rid of him quickly" (U 72). If this hypothesis concerning the origin of Bloom is valid, then, ironically, not even the man who springs from M'Coy wishes to acknowledge his socially. The picture is created of Bloom, who strives continually to break out of his isolation and loneliness, refusing fellowship to a likeness of himself.

Another person who appears in "Grace," Martin Cunningham, like so many characters in Joyce's books, appears to be a projection of what Joyce himself might have become had his career taken a different turn. Had not Shem, the self-exiled penman, overcome Shaun in Joyce's personality, Cunningham might have been the mature result. A Castle official, "sensible," "influential," and "well-informed," Cunningham has only to open this mouth to make a fool of himself. Because he conforms and stands for respectability in the smug social life of middle-class Dublin, his empty platitudes and weighty tautologies, like Shaun's in *Finnegans Wake*, are received in approving silence by his friends. Like Shaun, he is the good-natured, fair-haired boy, pleasantly dull.

There is some reason to believe that Joyce intended to suggest at least a partial similarity between Cunningham and himself. Both in "Grace" and in *Ulysses*, Joyce stresses the fact that "his friends bowed to his opinions and considered that his face was like Shakespeare's" (D 199–200). In Bloom's words too: "Martin Cunningham's large eyes . . . . Sympathetic human man he is. Intelligent. Like Shakespeare's face. Always a good word to say" (U 95). In the episode of the Kildare Street Library, however, it is Stephen-Joyce who is associated with Shakespeare. Thus, by a kind of equation, Cunningham equals Shakespeare equals Stephen-Joyce. Further support is lent to this possibility by parallels on the distaff side. Projections of Joyce – Gabriel Conroy, the unloved husband of several of *Pomes Penyeach*, Little Chandler – all are unhappy in their married life. Joyce spends the better part of an episode of *Ulysses* describing the hell of Shakespeare's life with Anne Hathaway. Also, he stresses the fact that Cunningham's sole disadvantage in the social life of his community is his unfortunate marriage to a shrewish, drunken woman. Martin's wife, according to Bloom, leads him "the life of the damned." In *Finnegans Wake*, as "Merkin Cornyngwham, the official out of the castle on pension," Cunningham reappears briefly. Joyce writes *finis* to his career by reporting him "completely drowned off Erin Isles . . . in the red sea . . . . The arzurian deeps o'er his humbodumbones sweeps." Poor Martin's drunken wife is also present, cashing in on her husband's death: "his widdy the giddy is wreathing her murmoirs as her gracest triput to the Grocery Trader's Manthly" (F 387).

In spite of the evident sarcasm of much of Joyce's portrait of Cunningham, the conforming Dubliner of whom he could not approve, Martin emerges as a likeable, if uninteresting, man. He is a steadying influence upon his companions, steering them away from mention of suicide in Bloom's hearing, for he knows that Bloom's father has committed suicide. He does his best to make light of the difference of opinion between Bloom and The Citizen. Though he believes that "our religion is *the* religion" and takes pride in declaring it, he is tolerant of the beliefs of others. The Church, in the person of Father Conmee, considers him a "good practical catholic: useful at mission time."

From "Grace" to *Ulysses*, Joyce's technique for presenting Cunningham alters markedly. No longer does the omniscient narrator etch out the descriptive details which the reader needs to orient himself; instead, the briefing of the reader is entrusted to the stream of consciousness of a principal character. In this way, the reader is informed not only of Cunningham but directly of how Cunningham appears to Bloom. Insight is obtained into the personalities of two characters simultaneously. This device marks an advance in technique quite remarkable, from the short stories to *Ulysses*.

The fabric of Joyce's literary accomplishment is sewn with such threads as this. So many threads are used to ensure the strength of the complicated and tightly meshed whole that it is often difficult to know where to stop in the unraveling. Joyce's employment of the imagery of the butcher store in "The Boarding House" would, if considered, be revelatory of a technique often used in the *Wake*. The father-son theme which is the backbone of "Ivy Day in the Committee Room" – with Parnell as the godlike father figure to the generation gathered around the fire in Wicklow Street – receives more intellectual treatment, in a different context, in the Scylla-Charybdis episode of *Ulysses* and returns to haunt the imagination as Earwicker gives way to his progeny. The funeral scenes in *Stephen Hero*, complete with toadlike cemetery priest, remind the reader of the Hades episode. Cads like Corley are given a genealogy in *Ulysses* and are allowed to play out their parts against the richer background of the long novel. Maria of "Clay," embodying characteristics of a witch and of the Virgin Mary, anticipates Molly Bloom in her triple role of Dublin soprano, Greek heroine, and feminine essence. The profusion of critical and interpretative comment is one evidence that the density of Joyce's canon is no longer underestimated.

Perspective is a dimension which must come slowly in evaluating contemporary writing, and it must come, of course, with detachment. Buffeted about for eighteen years by chilly indifference to his work from the practical public, Joyce was not entirely prepared for fame in 1922. Nine days after the publication of *Ulysses* on February 2 of that year, he writes excitedly to Robert McAlmon:

> The British Museum ordered a copy [of *Ulysses*] and so did the *Times* so that I advise you to go to confession for the last day cannot be far off. The *Dail Eireann* minister of propaganda called on me and wished to know if I intended to return to Ireland – to which I returned an evasive answer. He is proposing me, it seems, for the Nobel prize in his capacity of

cabinet minister as soon as the treaty is ratified at Westminster though not in the name of his cabinet. I will take on a small bet that if he does not change his mind when he sees the complete text he will lose his portfolio while I have not the faintest chance of being awarded the prize.[10]

Now, thirty-five years later, the task of seeing the "complete text" – but of seeing it whole – still offers a challenge.

(Page references are to the Modern Library edition and, in parentheses, to The Portable James Joyce, *The Viking Press, 1947.)*

THE SISTERS

p. 7 (19). *"The Sisters"*: This story in crude form was first published in *The Irish Homestead* on August 13, 1904. The significant alterations of fact and plot are discussed in Chapter III as well as in the notes below.

p. 7 (19). *the word gnomon*: perhaps a reference to the masonic order. This order is identified with geometry, with fixed axioms of belief, and with geometric symbols. Masons, it is believed, wanted the book suppressed. See Julian B Kaye's explanation in *A James Joyce Miscellany* (New York, 1957).

p. 9 (20). *Jack*: The *Irish Homestead* version reads "John." In the Slocum manuscript, "John" is crossed out and "Jack" is inserted in the margin.

p. 9 (20). *that Rosicrucian there*: this line does not appear in earlier versions. At the time he was writing this story, Joyce was interested in theosophy, secret societies, correspondences, etc. But he had sense of humor enough to smile at the dreamy-eyed, pimply faced, unathletic young men and women who belonged to AE's theosophical group. The boy of the story, introspective and timid, evokes the epithet. (See Gogarty, *Mourning Became Mrs. Spendlove*, pp. 53 ff.) Moreover, members of the Rosicrucian sect pretend to know what is happening in distant places. They seclude themselves and seek after true philosophy. This fits the description of the boy narrator and of Joyce himself. There is also the possibility, though more remote, that the word is a misspelling of "Rossacrucian," a follower of O'Donovan Rossa, whom Joyce mentions elsewhere in the volume. Rossa was an Irish revolutionary hero of Joyce's youth, a Fenian active in Ireland at the time when the action of "The Sisters" takes place.

p. 10 (22). *S. Catherine's Church*: Built 1852–58, it is on Meath Street, five blocks from St. Stephen's Green. I find no mention of St. Ita's Church in Dublin.

p. 14 (24–25). *his large hands . . . retaining a chalice*: A variation of this scene is evoked in the Circe episode of *Ulysses*. Mrs. Purefoy lies on an altar, "a chalice resting on her swollen belly."

p. 16 (26). *the "Freeman's General"*: misnomer for the *Freeman's Journal*, a Dublin newspaper to which Joyce submitted book reviews during his post-graduate days in Ireland. This newspaper was the chief rival of the *Irish Times*. In 1841 it "was acquired by a group of supporters of O'Connell's Repeal (of the Act of Union) policy, the chief of whom was John Gray – afterwards Sir John Gray – a Protestant of strong nationalist leanings." Later, it was passed on to his son, Edmund Dwyer Gray, "described by William O'Brien . . . as 'the most enterprising newspaperman Ireland ever produced.' But this enterprise was not in the political sphere. On the contrary the *Freeman* was always moderate and cautious to a fault . . . ." (Stephen J. Brown, *The Press in Ireland*, p. 36.)

p. 17 (27). *Irishtown:* slum section of Dublin. "Returning from Poolbeg light to Dublin, the road turns inland at the entrance to the Grand Canal Dock, leading to Ringsend and . . . southwards to the not very savoury Irishtown." (John Harvey, *Dublin,* p. 35.)

AN ENCOUNTER

p. 20 (29). *"An Encounter":* written by November, 1905.

p. 20 (29). *"The Union Jack," "Pluck,"* and *"The Halfpenny Marvel":* popular literature for boys issued during the eighteen-nineties by Alfred C. Harmsworth. *The Halfpenny Marvel* appeared in 1893, when Stephen-Joyce was eleven years old. It was published supposedly to kill the more sensational literature for boys, which had preceded it. The first number contained this message: "No more penny dreadfuls! These healthy stories of mystery, adventure, etc., will kill them." "At all the public schools," wrote Harmsworth, "there is a great rush for the Halfpenny Marvel." *The Union Jack* followed in 1894, and was also supposed to contain only "pure healthy tales." This publication, whose early stories were "mostly open-air tales of redskins, explorers, prospectors, sailors . . . ," did not cease operations until 1933. The third of the magazines, *Pluck,* also began publication in 1894. Its favorite theme concerned the adventures of three boys in foreign lands. (See E. S. Turner, *Boys Will Be Boys,* London: Michael Joseph, 1948, for the history of these periodicals.) Joyce mentions Harmsworth in the Aeolus episode of *Ulysses.* J. J. O'Molloy, speaking of former newspapermen, says: "Why not bring in Henry Grattan and Flood and Demosthenes and Edmund Burke? Ignatius Gallaher we all know and his Chapelizod boss, Harmsworth of the farthing press . . . . Sufficient for the day is the newspaper thereof" (U 137).

p. 20 (29). *mass . . . in Gardiner Street:* at St. Francis Xavier's, an imposing pillared church of the Jesuits, built 1829-32, near Eccles Street.

p. 22 (30). *National School boys:* not educated in a Catholic parochial school, but in schools established by the government. John of Tuam (see "Grace") fought them bitterly, fearing they would help to weaken the faith of Irish Catholic children.

p. 22 (31). *miching*: playing truant.

p. 22 (31). *the Pigeon House:* see above, Chapter II.

p. 24 (32). *the Vitriol Works*: Joyce refers here to The Dublin Vitriol Works Co., 17 Ballybough Road. As usual with this author, the location of this landmark is consistent with the itinerary of the characters.

p. 24 (32). *the Smoothing Iron*: I have been unable to identify this. It was probably a curious hill or rock formation so nicknamed by the children.

p. 25 (34). *Ringsend*: See Weston St. John Joyce, *The Neighbourhood of Dublin*, Chapter I.

p. 26 (34). *the Dodder:* "a charming little river, the Dodder, comes down out of the beautiful Glenasmole (or Thrushes Glen) and falls into the Liffey at the tideway." (Stephen Gwynn, *Dublin Old and New*, p. 11.) The Dodder today, however, is confined between artificial banks.

p. 27 (34). *jerry hat*: a hard round hat (ca. 1840–1870).

p. 28 (35). *totties*: sweethearts; it has also the connotation of "high-class" prostitutes.

p. 30 (37). *old josser:* an old roué; a fellow (with "old"). That the word "josser" can mean "god" in pidgin English should be considered.

ARABY

p. 33 (39). *"Araby"*: written by November, 1905.

p. 33 (39). *the Christian Brothers' School*: this school, on North Richmond Street, was founded in 1828. The patriot, and Joyce's relative, Daniel O'Connell, subscribed to the erection of the school and laid the foundation stone. The group of which the school is a part is also called the "O'Connell Schools" for boys. It trains boys from twelve to eighteen years of age. Childhood conditioning by his father and later independent observation had made Joyce almost despise the Christian Brothers and the sheep-like obedience which they appeared to exact from their willing students, young and immature. In *A Portrait*, Mr. Dedalus will not consider sending Stephen to a school run by Christian Brothers, mainly because that organization is inferior socially to the Jesuit group: "Christian Brothers be damned!

said Mr Dedalus. Is it with Paddy Stink and Mickey Mud?
No, let him stick to the jesuits . . . . Those are the fellows that
can get you a position" (P 78–79). Again in *A Portrait*, at a
crucial moment, when he is wondering whether he should have
refused a career leading to ordination, he tramps over a bridge
as a "squad of Christian Brothers" marches over it in the
opposite direction. He sees their "uncouth faces" and he feels
"shame and commiseration." He pities them for their regiment-
ation and ordinariness. Yet, significantly, he and they have
passed over the bridge to opposite shores (P 192–193). In
Ulysses, with much more detachment, Joyce sees the faults of
the Christian Brothers' schools. He has the unintelligent Corley
admit that even in such an easy school as that he "Got stuck
twice in the junior" (U 601). Joyce is haughtily reminiscent of
his father when he has the narrator in *Ulysses* say: "A band of
satchelled schoolboys crossed from Richmond street. All raised
untidy caps. Father Conmee greeted them more than once
benignly. Christian brother boys" (U 218).

p. 33 (39). *"The Abbot" by Walter Scott*: written in 1820, it deals
with Scotland and the captivity of Mary Queen of Scots at
Lochleven. The novel abounds in romance and in young,
beautiful women.

p. 33 (39). *"The Devout Communicant"*: the full title of this book is
*The Devout Communicant: or Pious Meditations and Aspirations for
the three days before and three days after receiving the Holy Eucharist.*
It appeared in 1813. The author, Pacificus Baker, is a man
whose identity has aroused considerable controversy. According to *DNB* he was a Provincial of the Order, and it has been
suggested that he received Gibbon into the Catholic Church
at the Sardinian Embassy chapel.

p. 33 (39). *"The Memoirs of Vidocq"*: the full title of this book,
written by Eugene F. Vidocq, and published in London in
1828–29, is *Memoirs of Vidocq, principal agent of the French police
until 1827: and now proprietor of the paper manufactory at Mandé.
Written by Himself.*

p. 35 (41). *O'Donovan Rossa*: (see note on *"that Rosicrucian there"*
under "The Sisters.") Rossa's actual name was Jeremiah
O'Donovan. He became a leader of the revolutionary Phoenix
Society and advocated "the most extreme and violent

measures." For this he was nicknamed "Dynamite Rossa." After living for a time in the United States, he returned to Ireland in 1863 to associate himself with "the Fenian organ, *The Irish People*. The paper was seized in 1865 and O'Donovan was held on a charge of treason-felony . . . sentenced to imprisonment for life, but . . . released . . . and banished . . . ." He returned to Ireland from the United States in 1891 and remained there till 1900. (See *Encyclopedia Americana*, 1943 edition, XXIII, 706.) Richmond Bridge, over the Liffey, has been renamed O'Donovan Rossa Bridge.

p. 39 (44). "*The Arab's Farewell to his Steed*": the poem is by the famous nineteenth-century personage, Mrs. Caroline Norton. It is known also as "The Arab's Farewell to his Horse." Its lines are incongruous in the mouth of a middle-aged Dubliner, for they take the form of an impassioned leave-taking by a young Arab of his horse, whom he had just sold to a stranger. The presence of the poem in the story is another reinforcement of the Oriental motif in *Dubliners*.

p. 39 (44). *down Buckingham Street towards the station*: in the northeast section of the city. The station referred to is the Amiens Street Station. The train crosses the Liffey at Tara Street and stops at Westland Row Station in central Dublin. A "few minutes" from this station was the Araby bazaar.

EVELINE

p. 42 (46). "*Eveline*": written probably in 1903 and published in *The Irish Homestead* on September 10, 1904.

p. 43 (47). *Blessed Margaret Mary Alacoque*: (1647–1690). She was a religious of the Visitation Order, Apostle of the Devotion to the Sacred Heart of Jesus. Born in France, she showed intense love of the Blessed Sacrament and preferred silence and prayer to childish amusements. Because of the tortures which she inflicted upon herself, she became paralyzed, but a miraculous cure occurred when she vowed to consecrate herself to a holy life. From this time on, except for a brief period of return to the world, from which she was rescued by a vision of a reproachful and suffering Christ, she devoted herself to a life of strict religious mortification of self. Whether Joyce intended any identification of the saint with Eveline, who also becomes paralyzed at the docks and is thus recalled to her drab, celibate life, is a matter for the reader to decide. Joyce was fond of the sound of the saint's name and the ease with which it could be punned upon. Mulligan, in *Ulysses*, prays to "Blessed Margaret Mary Anycock" (U 199), and traces of the name are in *Finnegans Wake*.

p. 45 (49). "*The Bohemian Girl*": an opera by William Balfe, the Irish composer, very popular in Dublin.

p. 46 (50). *Hill of Howth*: nine miles northeast of Dublin, on the seacoast. The hill is 560 feet high, and at its foot is a seaside resort. (See Weston St. John Joyce, *The Neighbourhood of Dublin* Chapter XXXI.)

p. 47 (50). *Derevaun Seraun*: these words seem to be crazed ravings, the meaning of which I have been unable to determine.

p. 47 (50). *North Wall*: the dock from which all sea passenger movement to and from Dublin occurred. George Moore, in *The Untilled Field*, portrays memorable scenes of greeting and farewell here.

AFTER THE RACE

p. 49 (52). "*After the Race*": This story appeared first in *The Irish Homestead* on December 17, 1904. Joyce made no revisions in it after that time, although Gorman records that the author wanted to rewrite it as late as August, 1906. (See Herbert Gorman, *James Joyce*, p. 169.)

p. 49 (52). *the Naas Road*: covers the distance from Naas, twenty miles west of Dublin, to Inchicore, the district south of Phoenix Park and the Liffey, on the western outskirts of the city.

p. 49 (52). *André Rivière . . . Villona*: These are the names of real people, acquaintances of Joyce in his student days in Paris. Rivière's name may have been borrowed from Jacques Rivière, a Parisian specialist in physiotherapy to whom Joyce brought a letter of introduction from a London doctor. Villona is a drinking companion of Joyce in 1902 in a café called the Carrefour de l'Odéon. (See Gorman, pp. 88, 100, 129.)

p. 53 (55). *the Bank*: the Bank of Ireland, an imposing eighteenth-century structure at the juncture of busy Dame Street, Grafton

Street, and the College Green of Trinity College, in the heart of Dublin.

p. 54 (56). *Routh*: Eugene Routh was also an acquaintance of Joyce in Paris in 1902.

p. 55 (56). *Stephen's Green*: a twenty-two-acre park in the center of Dublin. University College, Joyce's Alma Mater, is flanked by the Green.

p. 55 (57). *Kingstown Station*: Kingstown (now Dun Laoghaire) is on the seashore, seven miles southeast of Dublin, connected to metropolitan Dublin by the Railway.

TWO GALLANTS

p. 58 (59). *"Two Gallants"*: In a letter dated February 28, 1906, Joyce mentions completion of "Two Gallants" between November, 1905, and the date of writing. He then sent the story to publisher Grant Richards for insertion in the manuscript copy of *Dubliners*, the edition that was never published. The only trace of this abortive edition of 1906 is page proof of two pages from "Two Gallants," numbered page twelve and thirteen. A penciled note at the side of page 13 says, "We cannot print this/ [initials?] April 17, 1906." This sheet of page proof, now in the Houghton Library of Harvard University, differs from the final published version of the story in the unimportant alteration of four words; but also in the more interesting fact that the page-proof version lacks thirty-six consecutive lines that appear in *Dubliners*. The missing lines, beginning at the bottom of page 58 of the Modern Library edition with "Once or twice . . . ," end at the top of page 60 with "Corley ran his tongue along his upper lip." Though the Slocum-Cahoon bibliography speaks of these pages of proof as having been "considerably expanded" in the published version of the story (see Slocum-Cahoon, p. 13), I believe that the text of the story was substantially the same in the early and the published version but that the page proof is defective. In the first place, exactly one page, to the line, is added in the final version. This is hardly accidental. Also, page 12 of proof ends with a description of Lenehan: "His eyes, twinkling, with cunning enjoyment, glanced at every moment towards his companion's face." Page 13 of the proof, without any transition to Corley, begins with Corley's speech, though Corley is designated only by the pronoun "He," which belongs logically and grammatically to Lenehan. Since Joyce is careful not to confuse his pronoun reference, apparently his transitional section is omitted. It should be noted finally that the omitted section ends with a question: "And where did you pick her up, Corley?" The first sentence of page 13 of proof answers thus: "One night . . . I was going along . . . and I spotted a fine tart." Without the question, the answer is very abrupt, uncalled for, and inartistic.

p. 60 (60). *Dame Street*: Dublin Castle and City Hall are on this street.

p. 60 (61). *Donnybrook*: southern suburb of Dublin, close to the neighbourhood in which Joyce was born.

p. 60 (61). *Pim's*: a large Quaker dry goods store. AE worked here as an accountant and clerk. It was established in 1841 on George's Street, off Dame Street.

p. 62 (62). *girls off the South Circular*: South Circular Road is a long, curving highway which cuts across west central Dublin, roughly parallel to the Grand Canal.

p. 63 (63). *She's on the turf*: term applied from about 1860, to a prostitute.

p. 64 (64). *Nassau Street . . . Kildare Street*: Joyce is very careful to trace realistically the wanderings of the two "friends" through Dublin in this story.

p. 65 (64). *"Silent, O Moyle"*: one significant stanza of this poem by Thomas Moore contains these lines:

> *"Yet still in darkness doth Erin lie sleeping,*
> *Still doth the pure light its dawning delay!*
> *When will that day-star, mildly springing,*
> *Warm our isle with peace and love?"*

THE BOARDING HOUSE

p. 74 (71). *"The Boarding House"*: the finished story is dated, in manuscript draft, "1-7-05."

p. 74 (71). *a butcher's shop near Spring Gardens*: the Slocum manuscript at Yale University reads "in Fairview," which is in the northeastern section of Dublin near the Howth Road. The change may have been in line with the desire of the publisher to avoid identifying business establishments. If so, however, the change did not entirely accomplish its purpose, for a "Mr. James Mooney" is listed at number 3 Spring Garden Street in Thom's *Directory* for 1896. Both sections are close together.

p. 75 (72). *Hardwicke Street*: in the north central part of Dublin, above Parnell Square and in view of Eccles Street.

p. 75 (73). *vamped*: improvised.

p. 77 (74). *George's Church*: a little off Dorset Street. It is very close to Hardwicke Street so that its bells might easily have been heard by Mrs. Mooney in the boarding house. The church is Protestant. Several times during the day, on June 16, 1904, Mr. Bloom in *Ulysses* hears the bells of George's Church ring out, "loud dark iron."

p. 78 (75). *Short twelve at Marlborough Street:* refers to noon Mass at the Catholic Metropolitan Pro-Cathedral, just a short walk from Hardwicke Street.

A LITTLE CLOUD

p. 85 (80). *"A Little Cloud"*: Joyce wrote this story during February and March of 1906, in Trieste, and sent it to Grant Richards in July of 1906. It was not included in the original twelve stories of *Dubliners* submitted earlier.

p. 85 (80). *Gallaher had got on:* In the Aeolus episode of *Ulysses*, Joyce explains how Gallaher had got on. Editor Myles Crawford says: "Gallaher, that was a pressman for you. That was a pen. You know how he made his mark? I'll tell you. That was the smartest piece of journalism ever known. That was in eighty-one, sixth of May, time of the invincibles, murder in the Phoenix park." Then the editor becomes specific: "*New York World* cabled for a special on the murder. What did Ignatius Gallaher do? I'll tell you. Inspiration of genius. Cabled right away" (U 134–135).

p. 85 (80). *King's Inns*: North of the Liffey, in the center of Dublin, is this structure, equivalent to the Inns of Court in London. It is on Henrietta Street. Little Chandler, since he works here, is most likely a law clerk.

p. 87 (82). *Corless's*: No restaurant of this name appears to have existed in Dublin. However, Thom's *Directory* for 1896 lists on page 1711 this item: "Corless, Thomas, wine merchant and proprietor Burlington dining rooms, 24, 26 and 27 St. Andrew Street, oyster beds, Burrin, and 6 Church Lane." And later in the directory: "Burlington Restaurant and Oyster Saloons 27 St. Andrew St." This must be the restaurant Joyce has in mind.

p. 95 (88). *He summarized the vices of many capitals*: Gallaher's remarks, couched in the clichés of advertisements for pornographic literature, are paralleled by one of Stephen's speeches in the Circe episode of *Ulysses*: "Thousand places of entertainment to expenses your evenings with lovely ladies . . . perfect fashionable house very eccentric where lots cocottes beautiful dressed much about princesses like are dancing cancan and walking there parisian clowneries extra foolish for bachelors foreigns . . . . All chic womans which arrive full of modesty then disrobe and squeal loud . . ." (U 555.)

p. 101 (93). *Bewley's*: a chain-store group specializing in selling beverages and supplying light lunches. "Bewley's Oriental Cafes" (note the possible significance of the name) were located on Grafton Street, Westmorland Street and S. St. George Street.

p. 103 (95). *"Hushed are the winds"*: Byron's poem is called "On the Death of a Young Lady." It is the first poem in standard editions of the poet's works.

COUNTERPARTS

p. 106 (97). *"Counterparts"*: This story was written before December, 1905.

p. 106 (97). *Mr. Alleyne*: Joyce here may be satirizing his father's former employer, Henry Alleyn, who owned the Dublin and Chapelizod Distilling Company. John Stanislaus Joyce had been secretary of the Company. Thom's lists a "C. W. Alleyne, solicitor."

p. 109 (99). *O'Neill's shop*: Patrick O'Neill kept a pub at 1 Henry Street at this time.

p. 114 (104). *Terry Kelly's pawn-office in Fleet Street*: It was here that Joyce himself frequently repaired when he was in need of money during his student days. Padraic Colum, in *The Road round Ireland* (p. 318), tells of Joyce's attempt to redeem a pawn ticket and then to sell the redeemed merchandise, a set of Scott's Waverley novels. But because one of the novels was missing, bookseller George Webb advised Joyce and Colum to take them back to Terence Kelly's pawnshop and ask the proprietor to refund their money.

p. 115 (104). *Davy Byrne's*: the scene of part of the Lestrygonian episode of *Ulysses*. The pub is located at 21 Duke Street, between Trinity College and St. Stephen's Green.

p. 116 (105). *The Scotch House*: Like the other public houses in "Counterparts," this is the name of a real drinking place, one sometimes frequented by Joyce in the days surrounding his first trip to Paris. Writing of public houses in Dublin, Joyce says that they "are mentioned in four stories out of fifteen. In three of these stories the names are fictitious. In the fourth ("Counterparts") the names are real because the persons walked from place to place . . . ." (See Gorman, pp. 215–216.)

p. 117 (106). *Mulligan's in Poolbeg Street*: a real public house across the Liffey from the Custom House. James Mulligan, grocer, wine and spirit merchant, operated from 8 Poolbeg Street. (Thom's, 1896.)

p. 120 (108). *Shelbourne Road*: a southeast suburban street, near the slums of Irishtown.

CLAY

p. 123 (110). *"Clay"*: This story was written in Pola in November, 1904. Joyce first called it "Hallow Eve" and, under this title, submitted it to the *Literary World*, which rejected it. Later he changed the title and added the story to *Dubliners*.

p. 124 (111). *From Ballsbridge to the Pillar . . . from the Pillar to Drumcondra*: The trip takes Maria from southeast Dublin to northeast Dublin in forty minutes. Since all tram traffic in that city radiated from the Nelson Pillar on O'Connell Street, distances were usually measured in terms of minutes from the monument. This situation is substantially unchanged today in Dublin.

p. 124 (111). *"Dublin by Lamplight" laundry*: "Address – The Matron, 35, Ballsbridge terrace." (Thom's, 1896, p. 1326.) An interesting short discussion of Maria's relationship to the Donnelly family and to the Protestant Dublin by Lamplight laundry is available – Norman Holmes Pearson, "Joyce's Clay," *The Explicator*, VII, item 9 (October, 1948.)

p. 127 (113). *She got out of her tram at the Pillar*: Maria, or at least the type of frustrated virgin she represents, enters *Ulysses* as the double image of Anne Kearns and Florence MacCabe, the two husbandless women who enjoy spending their day off at the top of the Nelson Pillar. Perhaps Joyce is hinting at the relationship when he heads their story with the word "Dubliners." The descriptive phrases he uses may well be applied to Maria. "Two Dublin vestals . . . elderly and pious." Their poverty and concern over their meager savings is also reminiscent: "They shake out the threepenny bits and a sixpence and coax out the pennies . . . . They put on their bonnets and best clothes" to celebrate their day off. Even some of the details of the narrative agree with those of "Clay." Like Maria, they enter a bakery near the Pillar and buy several of the products. Here the narrative resemblance ends, though the sexual symbolism of the Pillar for the vestals is paralleled by the symbolism of clay which Maria gets in the party game. In both situations, only barrenness and sterility await the old ladies, regardless of the fond illusions of a fruitful holiday that they cherish.

There are further symbolic interweavings with *Dubliners*. Stephen tells how the two old women "take their umbrellas for fear it may come on to rain." Though this suggests a symbolic interpretation on several levels, most obviously it appears to parallel Gabriel's galoshes and the unknown man's macintosh – instruments for protection from life and nature. The old women enjoy life by seeing the "views of Dublin from the top of Nelson's pillar." Real life they repel by fortifying themselves with a covering against the rain, symbol of fertility, of regeneration, of life. The umbrella and the statue itself, which Stephen calls "the onehandled adulterer," seem roughly suggestive of the missing nutcracker and the corkscrew in "Clay." (See U 143–148.)

p. 132 (117). *"I Dreamt that I Dwelt"*: the words are by Alfred Bunn (1796–1860) and the music by William Balfe (1808–1870). Maria's error is the omission of two verses describing her as beset by suitors.

A PAINFUL CASE

p. 133 (118). *"A Painful Case"*: In the early draft, there is evidence
of considerable technical and stylistic uncertainty on Joyce's
part, which shows itself in the unusual amount of crossing out
and marginal addition. The intermediate draft is dated
"15–8–05." Except for unimportant alterations in vital statistics (names of people and places), this draft is very close to the
published version.

p. 133 (118). *Mr. James Duffy*: Probably coincidentally, this is
also the name of the publisher of many works of James Clarence
Mangan.

p. 133 (118). *Chapelizod*: village to the extreme west of Dublin,
adjoining Phoenix Park. The Earwicker family lives here in
Finnegans Wake.

p. 133 (118) *he could look into the disused distillery*: this may well have
been the firm of which Joyce's father was secretary. In John
Stanislaus's words: "I knew the place [Chapelizod] very well
for I was Secretary to the Distillery there for 3 or 4 years. It
was owned by the Dublin and Chapelizod Distilling Coy . . . ."
(*A James Joyce Yearbook*, 1949, p. 159.)

p. 133 (118). *the "Maynooth Catechism"*: This is the "Catechism
ordered by the National Synod of Maynooth . . . for General
Use throughout the Irish Church." It is more frequently used
than any other catechism in Ireland. "After a short Introduction on God and the creation of the world and on man and the
end of his creation, it treats in turn of the Creed, the Command-
ments, Prayers, and the Sacraments. The answers are short and
clear . . . ." ("Doctrine, Christian," *The Catholic Encyclopedia*,
V, 87.)

p. 134 (119). *Hauptmann's "Michael Kramer"*: See above, Chapter
II.

p. 134 (119). *a redeeming instinct in others*: the early manuscript
draft has "a redeeming instant in the lives his soul spurned."
Joyce had great difficulty with the writing of this paragraph
and revised the manuscript page until it is very difficult to
read the welter of marginal corrections and interpolations.

p. 135 (120). *an eating-house in George's Street*: maybe Bewley's.

p. 136 (121). *Sinico:* the name of Joyce's music master on the Continent.

p. 139 (123). *"Thus Spake Zarathustra"*: See above, Chapter II.

p. 140 (124). *"The Mail"*: a Tory newspaper which "opposed every national movement." Another newspaper in Ireland, *The Patriot,* commenting on *The Mail,* said: "In its pages Protestantism appears as a *fiend* of hatred instead of the religion of the God of charity, peace and goodwill." One must admire the care with which Joyce builds up every dimension of his characters, even to prescribing for them the newspaper which shall peep out of a pocket to reveal reading tastes in keeping with their personalities.

p. 141 (124). *the lonely road . . . from the [Phoenix] Park-gate to Chapelizod:* now called Chapelizod Road.

p. 141 (124). *Sydney Parade:* on the Dublin coast, directly south of Irishtown and the Pigeonhouse Fort. Kingstown lies a few miles to the south.

p. 141 (124). *the City of Dublin Hospital:* The early draft read "the morgue." The late draft has "Vincent's Hospital." St. Vincent's Hospital and Dispensary, on Stephen's Green East, was a denominational institution, opened by the Sisters of Charity in 1834. The City of Dublin Hospital, founded in 1832 and enlarged in 1893, is located on Upper Baggot Street. It is supported by voluntary contributions. It boasts that "Accidents and cases of emergency are received at all hours without recommendation." Perhaps this is the reason for Joyce's change of hospital name, since Mrs. Sinico was injured at night. He did not have in mind the distance of the two hospitals from the scene of the accident, for both are conveniently in the vicinity.

p. 142 (125). *P. Dunne:* The early draft reads "Kilbride."

p. 142 (125). *Mr. H. B. Patterson Finlay:* "Higgins" in the manuscript draft.

p. 146 (128). *Magazine Hill:* This refers probably to the location of the Magazine Fort, on what was formerly Thomas Hill, in Phoenix Park, of which Swift said:

> *Behold a proof of Irish sense,*
> *Here Irish wit is seen,*
> *When nothing's left that's worth defense,*
> *We build a magazine.*

L

The Magazine Wall in Phoenix Park is also the scene of furtive loves in the *Wake*. Here the soldiers spy on the Maggies and Earwicker blunders by (F 7).

p. 146 (129). *the laborious drone of the engine*: The manuscript drafts read much more explicitly, "melody of the engine, 'Emily Sinico, Emily Sinico, Emily Sinico.' " Even the stress marks to indicate the rhythm of the noise of the train are present.

IVY DAY IN THE COMMITTEE ROOM

p. 148 (129). *"Ivy Day in the Committee Room"*: The manuscript in the Yale-Slocum collection is dated 29 August, 1905. The custom of wearing a sprig of ivy in the lapel on October sixth in memory of Parnell's death is popular in Ireland. Ivy is also the symbol of regeneration.

p. 149 (130). *Royal Exchange Ward:* This was an actual ward in Dublin. It included in its jurisdiction several of the busiest streets in the neighborhood of centrally located University College.

p. 149 (130). *the Committee Room in Wicklow Street*: in the heart of Dublin's business section, adjoining Grafton and Nassau Streets.

p. 152 (133). *the Corporation*: "the Corporations . . . introduced . . . in the earlier stages were essentially defenses for maintaining English authority over a hostile people . . . . As affairs became more settled . . . successive Corporations more and more applied themselves to matters of local interest." After 1840 "Municipal Government . . . was vested in a Corporation consisting of the Lord Mayor, Aldermen and Councillors, who in turn elected a Lord Mayor each year. These elected representatives formed the Municipal Council."

p. 152 (133). *shoneens*: would-be gentlemen.

p. 153 (133). *kowtowing to a foreign king*: this strong language directed against The Crown was one of the issues which alienated Joyce from his early publishers. Gorman's book contains details of the dispute.

p. 157 (136). *hillsiders and fenians:* nicknames for patriotic political agitation groups in Ireland.

p. 157 (137). *the Castle*: the official buildings occupied formerly by the British governors in Dublin and by their Irish associates. These authorities were known familiarly as "The Castle." The Committee Room is only two streets from it.

p. 157 (137). *Major Sirr*: a leader in combatting the conspiracy for an insurrection in 1798. Because the plot was denounced by informers, it did not succeed. Major Sirr has become notorious for his methods of spying and for the brutality of the police under his supervision. "Major Sirr's title was not a military one, but an abbreviated form of 'Town Major,' a corporate office long since abolished." (Weston St. John Joyce, *The Neighbourhood of Dublin*, p. 161.)

p. 160 (139). *Mansion House*: the residence of the Lord Mayor of Dublin on Dawson Street in central Dublin.

p. 168 (146). *"The Death of Parnell"*: It has been suggested that Joyce is here playfully satirizing the tone of his own first published work, the childhood political effort no longer extant, called "Et Tu, Healy!"

p. 170 (148). *When he had finished his recitation there was a silence:* Joyce found it a useful technique to show the effect of former dignity and greatness upon shabby, cynical modern Dubliners. The sentimental, rhetorical poem is his medium in "Ivy Day." In the Aeolus episode of *Ulysses*, the technique is reintroduced. This audience is the flippant, talkative group of newspapermen and pseudo-intellectuals in the newspaper office. Professor MacHugh recalls the "finest display of oratory I ever heard . . . a speech made by John F. Taylor . . ." As MacHugh repeats what he remembers of the speech, "His listeners held their cigarettes poised to hear . . . . Noble words coming." The speech is verbose, in the best traditions of academic oratory: "Great was my admiration in listening to the remarks addressed to the youth of Ireland a moment since by my learned friend. It seemed to me that I had been transported into a country far away from this country . . . ." Thus the speech starts; it goes on to reiterate the Moses theme of *Ulysses*. When MacHugh ends his recapitulation of the speech, "He ceased and looked at them, enjoying silence." That line ends the section. It is very much like the final remark of the author at the finish of "Ivy Day." "Mr. Crofton said that it was a very fine piece of writing." (See U 139–141.)

A MOTHER

p. 171 (148). "*A Mother*": this story was completed before the end of 1905. A draft of it in the Yale-Slocum collection differs from the published version only in the substitution of a dozen or so synonyms in the latter. The few changes made seem to be in the direction of simplification of diction and structure.

p. 171 (148). *Eire Abu*: an Irish patriotic slogan and exhortation.

p. 172 (150). *Skerries . . . Howth . . . Greystones*: summer resorts within a few miles of Dublin, on the seashore. Howth is closest to Dublin, only nine miles by tram. The other two resorts, both about eighteen miles from the city, have become more and more popular as bathing places during this century.

p. 173 (150). *the Antient Concert Rooms*: on what is now Pearse Street, near Westland Row Station. George Moore describes the place memorably as it was at this time: "A truly suitable place for a play by Edward Martyn [whose *The Heather Field* and other plays are in the drab, dismal Ibsen tradition] . . . . The long passage leading to the rooms seemed to be bringing me into a tomb. Nothing very renascent about this, I said, pushing my way through the spring doors into a lofty hall with a balcony and benches down the middle, and there were seats along the walls placed so that those who sat on them would have to turn their heads to see the stage, a stage that had been constructed hurriedly by advancing some rudely painted wings and improvising a drop curtain

". . . the melancholy of this dim hall I had never seen before . . . ." (*Hail and Farewell*, I, p. 75.) In placing the characters of his story in such a setting, Joyce is better able to suggest the paralysis of art in Dublin against as unbeautiful a background as ever a theater offered.

p. 174 (151). *Brown Thomas's*: This Grafton Street shop boasts that it has been "famous for 100 years for Irish Laces and Irish Linens . . . of best quality."

p. 179 (155). *the opera of "Maritana"*: in 1882, the year of Joyce's birth, the Carl Rosa Opera Company sang *Maritana*, by William Wallace, at the Gaiety Theatre.

p. 180 (155). *the Feis Ceoil*: an annual festival of music held in Dublin. In 1904, Joyce participated on the same program as

John McCormack. He was doing well and seemed assured of some prize, when he suddenly discovered that he had to sing at sight a selection handed to him on the platform. He refused to do so – and stalked off contemptuously. This episode is recorded in many places. (See Gorman, pp. 120 ff.)

GRACE

p. 190 (163). *"Grace"*: written before the end of 1905. The draft in the Yale-Slocum collection differs very little from the published version.

p. 193 (166). *an outsider*: a cab.

p. 194 (166). *the Ballast Office*: home of the Ballast Board, founded in 1707 to supervise harbor development in Dublin and vicinity.

p. 195 (167). *the great Blackwhite:* I have been unable to trace this name to its source. It is possible that here Joyce was inventing the myth of the successful salesman.

p. 196 (168). *Glasnevin Road*: in a suburb of northern Dublin, celebrated in the Hades episode of *Ulysses* for its cemetery.

p. 198 (170). *a draper's shop in Glasgow*: the manuscript copy reads "Galway." This Irish city is the home of Joyce's wife, Nora, and of Gretta Conroy in "The Dead."

p. 198 (170). *he would walk to the end of Thomas Street and back:* One wonders why Joyce picked a street so close to Mr. Kernan's office in Crowe Street if he wished to give the impression of extraordinary distance. Perhaps he meant to indicate the distance from Kernan's home to Thomas Street.

p. 199 (170): *Mr. M'Coy*: in the manuscript version, the name is invariably spelled "McCoy."

p. 120 (172). *The Irish Times:* "It was the first penny newspaper in Ireland . . . The *Irish Times* was from the start and has consistently remained the organ of the Protestant interest in Ireland, its politics being Conservative or Unionist. It steadily opposed all the national movements. It afforded a platform . . . for all those . . . whose first allegiance was to England or whose principal preoccupation was the maintenance of the existing order . . . ." (Stephen Brown, *The Press in Ireland*, p. 34.)

p. 202 (173). *"bona-fide" travellers:* Since 1921, Sunday opening is restricted to five hours in England, generally 12–2 p.m. and 7–10 p.m. Pubs are shut in Wales and N. Ireland and one can't get a drink, officially. Scotland and Eire still have the "bona-fide travellers" rule.

p. 205 (175). *These yahoos:* This Swiftian word is the only direct reference to Swift in *Dubliners*. Later, Joyce was to use Swift's life and work extensively in *Ulysses* and *Finnegans Wake*.

p. 206 (176). *"We can meet in M'Auley's"*: Bloom, in *Ulysses*, deprecates the location of this establishment. "Good house, however: just the end of the city traffic. For instance M'Auley's down there: n.g. as position. Of course if they ran a tramline along the North Circular from the cattle market to the quays value would go up like a shot" (U 57–58).

p. 209 (178). *"The Irish priesthood is honoured all the world over."*: Mr. Cunningham's remark, seconded by M'Coy's follow-up statement: "Not like some of the other priesthoods on the continent . . . unworthy of the name," shows Joyce laughing at smug Irish insularity. He laughs again in a very similar exchange of patriotic views in the Eumaeus episode of *Ulysses*. A veteran and a cabby discuss Ireland:

> – Who's the best troops in the army? the grizzled old veteran irately interrogated. And the best jumpers and racers? And the best admirals and generals we've got? Tell me that.
> – The Irish for choice, retorted the cabby . . .
> – That's right, the old tarpaulin corroborated. The Irish catholic peasant. He's the backbone of our empire. (U 625)

p. 211 (180). *Orangeman:* a member of a society organized in the north of Ireland in 1795 for the support of the Protestant religion. Calling Crofton by this name probably implies no fixed and formal membership but simply identifies his religious belief.

p. 212 (181). *Pope Leo XIII:* Mr. Cunningham knows the high points in the career of the pope, who was born March 2, 1810 and was educated in a Jesuit college. He was both scholar and poet. In political matters, he allowed the Irish church leaders to carry out their own policies, though, as in 1888, he denounced some of their methods. He considered himself a prisoner at the Vatican.

p. 213 (182). *oxter*: arm.

p. 214–215 (183). *when the Pope speaks "ex cathedra"* . . . *he is infallible*: This doctrine was defined in 1870 in a Vatican council under Pius IX. When the Pope speaks in "discharge of the office of pastor and doctor of all Christians," he speaks infallibly.

p. 215 (184). *a German cardinal by the name of Dolling . . . or Dowling*: Mr. Cunningham is confused. The man's name was really Professor Dollinger of Munich. He was a bishop, not a cardinal, and he left the church in September, 1871.

p. 215 (184). *John MacHale*: (1791–1881), Archbishop of Tuam. Scenes of brutality towards the poor, on the part of the police and the military so impressed him in childhood that he stood forward as a champion of the underprivileged. He attended the large seminary of Maynooth. Later he became a friend of Daniel O'Connell and, like the former, constantly preached for reform, especially of the penal code, as excessively brutal to Catholics. He caught the public eye with a series of vigorous articles in the *Freeman's Journal*, and was eventually made Archbishop of Tuam over the strenuous objections of the authorities in England. As Archbishop, he condemned the National Schools as tending to weaken the faith of Catholic children; and he helped to found the Christian Brother schools. In addition, he organized relief activities for the poor and aged in the famine of 1846–47. In spite of his patriotic activities, however, he was against the violent tactics of such organizations as the Young Ireland party. Mr. Cunningham dramatizes John's reaction to the announcement of papal infallibility, but he has the facts correct. John was against the *immediate* definition of the infallibility dogma; but once it was defined, he accepted it.

p. 217 (185) *Sir John Gray's statue. Edmund Dwyer Gray was speaking*: the Yale-Slocum manuscript first read "Smith O'Brien's statue" and prefaced Edmund Dwyer Gray's name with the adjective "Young." But both these original names are crossed out and the published version substituted.

Smith O'Brien (1803–1864) was an Irish political insurgent and head of the Young Ireland party, who joined with Daniel

O'Connell for the Repeal of Union with England. He took part in the revolt of 1848, was sentenced to die, but later was transported and finally pardoned.

Sir John Gray (1816–1875) was proprietor of the patriotic Home Rule paper which took a relatively moderate position, the *Freeman's Journal*. (See above, note on the "Freeman's General".) His statue stands on wide, graceful O'Connell Street, near a statue of his fellow patriot, Smith O'Brien. Both statues were done by Sir Thomas Farrell.

The death of John Gray's son, Edmund Dwyer Gray, the journalist, is recorded sadly, with appropriate verses and a portrait, in the cartoon supplement to the *Freeman's Journal* for 1888.

p. 221 (189). *"For the children of this world"*: Luke, XVI, 8.

THE DEAD

p. 224 (190). *"The Dead"*: written in March, 1907, after the subject had been thought out for a considerable time. The manuscript in the Yale-Slocum collection is incomplete.

p. 224 (190). *Miss Kate*: Joyce's great-aunt and godmother, Miss Callanan, is the Aunt Kate of this *novella*.

p. 225 (191). *Usher's Island*: on the Liffey in central Dublin.

p. 225 (191). *Adam and Eve's*: a church on the Liffey mentioned in the first sentence of the *Wake*.

p. 226 (192). *"O, Mr. Conroy"*: Always on the lookout for indirect ways to suggest his themes, Joyce borrowed the name of his main character, Gabriel Conroy, from the title of Bret Harte's novel of California adventure, *Gabriel Conroy*. He was attracted to this novel, published in 1871, probably by its long, rhetorical description of snow, which succeeds in obliterating all signs of human life. By working back from the name of Joyce's hero, to that of Harte's, and then to the latter's handling of the snow motif, the reader may understand better, and must certainly appreciate more fully, Joyce's story of "The Dead."

Harte's description of the snow, on the first page of his novel, is couched in rhythmical prose that Joyce seems to echo at the end of his story. This from *Gabriel Conroy*:

> *Snow. Everywhere. As far as the eye could reach – fifty miles, looking southward from the highest white peak, – filling ravines*

*and gulches, and dropping from the walls of cañons in white
shroud-like drifts, fashioning the dividing ridge into the likeness
of a monstrous grave . . . . Snow lying everywhere over the
California Sierras . . . .*

*It had been snowing for ten days: snowing in finely granulated
powder, in damp spongy flakes, in thin feathery plumes, snowing
from a leaden sky steadily, snowing fiercely . . . . But always
silently . . . .*

In Harte's novel the heroine's name is "Grace," a variant of
the name of Joyce's heroine, Gretta. (See Gerhard Friedrich,
"Bret Harte as a Source for James Joyce's 'The Dead,'"
Philological Quarterly, XXXIII (1954), 442–444.)

p. 230 (195). *Monkstown*: suburb in the southeast section of
Dublin.

p. 231 (197). *Christy Minstrels*: a selection of songs and ballads
sung and popularized by this group in 1891 was issued at the
end of that year by C. Sheard & Co., Music Publishers. The
songs listed include "Moonlight will come again," "With all
her faults I love her still," and "Goin' from the cotton fields."

p. 232 (197). *the Gresham*: a luxury hotel on O'Connell Street.
The ability of the Conroys to stop there, even for one evening,
indicates their more than satisfactory financial condition. Even
today the hotel ranks with the best in Ireland.

p. 239 (203). Balbriggan: a city twenty miles north of Dublin.

p. 240 (204). *The Daily Express*: "*The Irish Times* though the best
was not the first Irish newspaper of its kind . . . . it had been
preceded a few years by the *Daily Express*, 1851–1921, which
announced its policy as being 'To reconcile the rights and im-
pulses of Irish nationality with the demands and obligations of
imperial dominion: The emphasis was to be laid on the development of industrial resources in the hope of joining Protestant
and Roman Catholic in that new field of endeavour.' It was all
along a Conservative paper, opposed to the national struggle."
(Stephen J. Brown, *The Press in Ireland*, p. 35.) It is not strange,
if this description is accurate, that Miss Ivors, the militant
patriot and Gaelic Leaguer, did not approve of Gabriel's book
reviewing for the *Express*.

p. 241 (204). *Webb's or Massey's on Aston's Quay*: these booksellers kept bookshops in Dublin during this period, George Webb on Crampton Quay and Edward Massy [*sic*] at 6 Aston's Quay.

p. 246 (208). *the Wellington Monument*: at the eastern end of Phoenix Park.

p. 247 (209). *"Arrayed for the Bridal"*: the music of this song is from Bellini's *I Puritani*. The words were written by George Linley. Since the words are significant and completely appropriate to the mood of the *novella*, and since Joyce does not give them, I reproduce them here:

> *Array'd for the bridal, in beauty behold her,*
> *A white wreath entwineth a forehead more fair;*
> *I envy the zephyrs that softly enfold her, enfold her,*
> *And play with the locks of her beautiful hair.*
> *May life to her prove full of sunshine and love,*
> *   full of love, yes! yes! yes!*
> *Who would not love her*
> *Sweet star of the morning! shining so bright,*
> *Earth's circle adorning, fair creature of light,*
> *Fair creature of light.*

p. 251 (212). *Beannacht libh*: Gaelic for "farewell" or "my blessing be with you."

p. 254 (215). *Theatre Royal*: two blocks north of Trinity College.

p. 255 (216). *Tietjens, Ilma de Murzka, Campanini, the great Trebelli, Giuglini, Ravelli, Aramburo*: Joyce knew his opera stars. Italo Campanini (1846–1896) was a brilliant operatic tenor who made his London debut in 1872 after achieving success on the Continent. His most successful role, perhaps, was in *Lucrezia Borgia*, a favourite in Dublin. Even Mr. Browne in *Dubliners* (p. 256) longs for a revival of that opera. Joyce's father mentions Campanini as "a great Italian singer [who] . . . came to Dublin a few times. He had a very fine voice; he was a big awkward man." (*James Joyce Yearbook*, 1949, p. 164.)

Therese Tietjens (1831–1877) was a German dramatic soprano. She came to London in 1858 and remained a favorite there until her death, playing at Drury-Lane, Covent Garden, and touring the country.

Ilma di Murska (1836–1889) was also a dramatic soprano. After meeting with great success all over the world, she committed suicide.

Zelia Trebelli (1838–1892) was a mezzo-soprano, born in Paris. London greeted her efforts with great acclaim. Aramburo and Guiglini were nineteenth-century tenors who sang in England for a time.

p. 257 (218). *Mount Melleray*: in southern Ireland. A celebrated Trappist monastery here has a guesthouse for visitors. It is in Cappoquin, Munster.

p. 260 (219). *Fifteen Acres*: the name given to the southwestern section of Phoenix Park.

p. 267 (225). *King Billy's statue*: before College Green and to the right of the Bank of Ireland stands the statue of King William III. The monarch is depicted riding a horse.

p. 285 (239). *Oughterard*: a small tree-laden village near Galway.

p. 288 (242). *the Bog of Allen*: a dreary waste where Kildare and Meath meet, south of Dublin.

p. 288 (242). *Michael Furey*: The reason why Joyce selected the names of Gabriel and Michael, two archangels, as rivals in love, is not clear. The Yale-Slocum manuscript shows Joyce undecided whether to spell Michael's last name "Fury" or "Furey."

APPENDIX B *A list of the characters in* Dubliners
whose names are mentioned in Ulysses

(Characters who have speaking roles in Ulysses *are designated by an asterisk preceding the name. Characters from* Dubliners *who are merely spoken of or thought of in* Ulysses *are designated by the following mark: (-*). The precise page references to the text of* Ulysses *on which each name appears may be obtained from Miles Hanley,* Word Index to James Joyce's Ulysses, *University of Wisconsin Press, 1937.)*

CHARACTERS COMMON TO "DUBLINERS" AND "ULYSSES"

-* Alleyne, Mr. (Counterparts)
-* Alacoque, Margaret Mary (Eveline)
-* Atkinson (Ivy Day)
 * Burke, O'Madden (A Mother)

* Conroy, Constantine (The Dead)
-* Conroy, Gabriel (The Dead)
-* Conroy, Gretta (The Dead)
 * Corley (Two Gallants)
 * Cowley, Alderman (Ivy Day)
 * Crofton (Ivy Day; Grace)
-* Crosbie, Mr. (Counterparts)
 * Cunningham, Martin (Grace)
-* D'Arcy, Bartell (The Dead)
-* Doran, Mr. (The Boarding House)
 * Flynn, Nosey (Counterparts)
-* Fogarty, Mr. (Grace)
-* Gallaher, Ignatius (A Little Cloud)
-* Gray, Sir John (Grace)
 * Holohan (Two Gallants; A Mother)
 * Hynes, Joe (Ivy Day)
-* Kearney, Kathleen (A Mother; The Dead)
 * Kernan, Tom (Grace)
 * Lenehan (Two Gallants)
 * Leonard, Paddy (Counterparts)
 * Lyons, Bantam (The Boarding House; Ivy Day)
 * M'Coy, C. P. (Grace)
-* Mooney, Jack (The Boarding House)
-* Mooney, Mrs. (The Boarding House)
-* Mooney, Polly (The Boarding House)
-* Morkan, Julia (The Dead)
-* Morkan, Kate (The Dead)
-* Peake (Counterparts)
 * Power, Jack (Grace)
-* Rossa, O'Donovan (Araby)
-* Sheridan, Mr. (The Boarding House)
-* Sinico, Emily (A Painful Case)
-* Sirr, Major (Ivy Day)

APPENDIX C *First printed version of James Joyce's*
"The Sisters" from The Irish Homestead *1904*
It is signed Stephen Daedalus

Three nights in succession I had found myself in Great Britain-street at that hour, as if by Providence. Three nights also I had raised my eyes to that lighted square of window and speculated. I seemed to understand that it would occur at night. But in spite of the Providence that had led my feet, and in spite of the reverent curiosity of my eyes, I had discovered nothing. Each night the square was lighted in the same way, faintly and evenly. It was not the light of candles, so far as I could see. Therefore, it had not yet occurred.

On the fourth night at that hour I was in another part of the city. It may have been the same Providence that led me there – a whimsical kind of Providence to take me at a disadvantage. As I went home I wondered was that square of window lighted as before, or did it reveal the ceremonious candles in whose light the Christian must take his last sleep. I was not surprised, then, when at supper I found myself a prophet. Old Cotter and my uncle were talking at the fire, smoking. Old Cotter is the old distiller who owns the batch of prize setters. He used to be very interesting when I knew him first, talking about "faints" and "worms." Now I find him tedious.

While I was eating my stirabout I heard him saying to my uncle:

"Without a doubt. Upper storey – (he tapped an unnecessary hand at his forehead) – gone."

"So they said. I never could see much of it. I thought he was sane enough."

"So he was, at times," said old Cotter.

I sniffed the "was" apprehensively, and gulped down some stirabout.

"Is he better, Uncle John?"

"He's dead."

"O . . . he's dead?"

"Died a few hours ago."

"Who told you?"

"Mr. Cotter here brought us the news. He was passing there."

"Yes, I just happened to be passing, and I noticed the window . . . you know."

"Do you think they will bring him to the chapel?" asked my aunt.

"Oh, no, ma'am. I wouldn't say so."

"Very unlikely," my uncle agreed.

So old Cotter had got the better of me for all my vigilance of three nights. It is often annoying the way people will blunder on what you have elaborately planned for. I was sure he would die at night.

The following morning after breakfast I went down to look at the little house in Great Britain-street. It was an unassuming shop registered under the vague name of "Drapery." The drapery was principally children's boots and umbrellas, and on ordinary days there used to be a notice hanging in the window, which said "Umbrellas recovered." There was no notice visible now, for the shop blinds were drawn down and a crape bouquet was tied to the knocker with white ribbons. Three women of the people and

O, King of Glory, is it not a great change
Since I was a young man, long, long ago?
When the heat of the sun made my face glow
  As I cut the grass, on a fine cloudless day;
Fair girls laughing
  All through the field raking hay,
Merry in the fragrant morning,
  And the sound of their voices like music in the air.

The bees were after the honey,
  Taking it to their nests among the hay,
Flying against us nimbly and merrily,
  And disappearing from sight with small keen buzz.
And the butterflies on the thistles,
  And on the meadow daisies, and from flower to flower,
On light wing lying and rising up,
  Moving through the air—they were fine.

The blackbird and the thrush were in the small nut wood,
  Making sweet music like the songs of the bards,
And the sprightly lark with a song in her little mouth
  Poising herself in the air aloft.
The beautiful thrush was on top of the branch,
  His throat stretched out in melodious song.
And, O, God of Grace, it was fine to be
  In beauteous Ireland at that time!

OUR WEEKLY STORY.

THE SISTERS.

By Stephen Dædalus.

Three nights in succession I had found myself in Great Britain-street at that hour, as if by Providence. Three nights also I had raised my eyes to that lighted square of window and speculated. I seemed to understand that it would occur at night. But in spite of the Providence that had led my feet, and in spite of the reverent curiosity of my eyes, I had discovered nothing. Each night the square was lighted in the same way, faintly and evenly. It was not the light of candles, so far as I could see. Therefore, it had not yet occurred.

On the fourth night at that hour I was in another part of the city. It may have been the same Providence that led me there—a whimsical kind of Providence to take me at a disadvantage. As I went home I wondered was that square of window lighted as before, or did it reveal the ceremonious candles in whose light the Christian must take his last sleep. I was not surprised, then, when at supper I found myself a prophet. Old Cotter and my uncle were talking at the fire, smoking. Old Cotter is the old distiller who owns the batch of prize setters. He used to be very interesting when I knew him first, talking about "faints" and "worms." Now I find him tedious.

While I was eating my stirabout I heard him saying to my uncle:

"Without a doubt. Upper storey—(he tapped an unnecessary hand at his forehead)—gone."

"So they said. I never could see much of it. I thought he was sane enough."

"So he was, at times," said old Cotter.

I sniffed the "was" apprehensively, and gulped down some stirabout.

"Is he better, Uncle John?"

"He's dead."

"O . . . he's dead?"

"Died a few hours ago."

"Who told you?"

"Mr. Cotter here brought us the news. He was passing there."

"Yes, I just happened to be passing, and I noticed the window . . . you know."

"Do you think they will bring him to the chapel?" asked my aunt.

"Oh, no, ma'am. I wouldn't say so."

"Very unlikely," my uncle agreed.

So old Cotter had got the better of me for all my vigilance of three nights. It is often annoying the way people will blunder on what you have elaborately planned for. I was sure he would die at night.

The following morning after breakfast I went down to look at the little house in Great Britain-street. It was an unassuming shop registered under the vague name of "Drapery." The drapery was principally children's boots and umbrellas, and on ordinary days there used to be a notice hanging in the window, which said "Umbrellas recovered." There was no notice visible now, for the shop blinds were drawn down and a crape bouquet was tied to the knocker with white ribbons. Three women of the people and a telegram boy were reading the card pinned on the crape. I also went over and read :—"July 2nd, 189— The Rev. James Flynn (formerly of St. Ita's Church), aged 65 years. R.I.P."

Only sixty-five! He looked much older than that. I often saw him sitting at the fire in the close dark room behind the shop, nearly smothered in his great coat. He seemed to have almost stupefied himself with heat, and the gesture of his large trembling hand to his nostrils had grown automatic. My aunt, who is what they call good-hearted, never went into the shop without bringing him some High Toast, and he used to take the packet of snuff from her hands, gravely inclining his head for sign of thanks. He used to sit in that stuffy room for the greater part of the day from early morning, while Nannie (who is almost stone deaf) read out the newspaper to him. His other sister, Eliza, used to mind the shop. These two old women used to look after him, feed him, and clothe him. The clothing was not difficult, for his ancient, priestly clothes were quite green with age, and his dogskin slippers were everlasting. When he was tired of hearing the news he used to rattle his snuff-box on the arm of his chair to avoid shouting at her, and then he used to make believe to read his Prayer Book. Make believe, because, when Eliza brought him a cup of soup from the kitchen, she had always to waken him.

As I stood looking up at the crape and the card that bore his name I could not realise that he was dead. He seemed like one who could go on living for ever if he only wanted to; his life was so methodical and uneventful. I think he said more to me than to anyone else. He had an egoistic contempt for all women-folk, and suffered all their services to him in polite silence. Of course, neither of his sisters were very intelligent. Nannie, for instance, had been reading out the newspaper to him every day for years, and could read tolerably well, and yet who always spoke of it as the *Freeman's General*. Perhaps he found me more intelligent, and honoured me with words for that reason. Nothing, practically nothing, ever occurred to remind him of his former life (I mean friends or visitors), and still he could remember every detail of it in his own fashion. He had studied at the college in Rome, and he taught me to speak Latin in the Italian way. He often put me through the responses of the Mass, he smiling often and pushing huge pinches of snuff up each nostril alternately. When he smiled he used to uncover his big, discoloured teeth, and let his tongue lie on his lower lip. At first this habit of his used to make me feel uneasy. Then I grew used to it.

That evening my aunt visited the house of mourning and took me with her. It was an oppressive summer evening of faded gold. Nannie received us in the hall, and, as it was no use saying anything to her, my aunt shook hands with her for all. We followed the old woman upstairs and into the dead-room. The room, through the lace end of the blind, was suffused with dusky golden light, amid which the candles looked like pale, thin flames. He had been coffined. Nannie gave the lead, and we three knelt down at the foot of the bed. There was no sound in the room for some minutes except the sound of Nannie's mutterings—for she prays noisily. The fancy came to me that the old priest was smiling as he lay there in his coffin.

But, no. When we rose and went up to the head of the bed I saw that he was not smiling. There he lay solemn and copious in his brown habit, his large hands loosely retaining his rosary. His face was very grey and massive, with distended nostrils and circled with scanty white fur. There was a heavy odour in the room—the flowers.

We sat downstairs in the little room behind the shop, my aunt and I and the two sisters. Nannie sat in a corner and said nothing, but her lips moved from speaker to speaker with a painfully intelligent motion. I said nothing either, being too young, but my aunt spoke a good deal, for she is a bit of a gossip—harmless.

"Ah, well! he's gone!"

"To enjoy his eternal reward, Miss Flynn, I'm sure. He was a good and holy man."

"He was a good man, but, you see . . . he was a disappointed man. . . . You see, his life was, you might say, crossed."

"Ah, yes! I know what you mean."

"Not that he was anyway mad, as you know yourself, but he was always a little queer. Even when we were all growing up together he was queer. One time he didn't speak hardly for a month. You know, he was that kind always."

"Perhaps he read too much, Miss Flynn?"

"O, he read a good deal, but not latterly. But it was his scrupulousness, I think, affected his mind. The duties of the priesthood were too much for him."

"Did he . . . peacefully?"

"O, quite peacefully, ma'am. You couldn't tell when the breath went out of him. He had a beautiful death, God be praised."

"And everything . . . ?"

"Father O'Rourke was in with him yesterday and gave him the Last Sacrament."

"He knew then?"

"Yes; he was quite resigned."

Nannie gave a sleepy nod and looked ashamed.

"Poor Nannie," said her sister, "she's worn out. All the work we had, getting in a woman, and laying him out; and then the coffin and arranging about the funeral. God knows we did all we could, as poor as we are. We wouldn't see him want anything at the last."

"Indeed you were both very kind to him while he lived."

"Ah, poor James; he was no great trouble to us. You wouldn't hear him in the house no more than now. Still I know he's gone and all that. . . . I won't be bringing him in his soup any more, nor Nannie reading him the paper, nor you, ma'am, bringing him his snuff. How he liked that snuff! Poor James!"

"O, yes, you'll miss him in a day or two more than you do now."

Silence invaded the room until memory reawakened it, Eliza speaking slowly—

"It was that chalice he broke. . . . Of course, it was all right. I mean it contained nothing. But still . . . They say it was the boy's fault. But poor James was so nervous, God be merciful to him."

"Yes, Miss Flynn, I heard that . . . about the chalice. . . He . . . his mind was a bit affected by that."

"He began to mope by himself, talking to no one, and wandering about. Often he couldn't be found. One night he was wanted, and they looked high up and low down and couldn't find him. Then the clerk suggested the chapel. So they opened the chapel (it was late at night), and brought in a light to look for him. . . And there, sure enough, he was, sitting in his confession-box in the dark, wide awake, and laughing like softly to himself. Then they knew something was wrong."

"God rest his soul!"

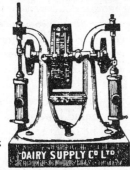

a telegram boy were reading the card pinned on the crape. I also went over and read: – "July 2nd, 189– The Rev. James Flynn (formerly of St. Ita's Church), aged 65 years. R.I.P."

Only sixty-five! He looked much older than that. I often saw him sitting at the fire in the close dark room behind the shop, nearly smothered in his great coat. He seemed to have almost stupefied himself with heat, and the gesture of his large trembling hand to his nostrils had grown automatic. My aunt, who is what they call good-hearted, never went into the shop without bringing him some High Toast, and he used to take the packet of snuff from her hands, gravely inclining his head for sign of thanks. He used to sit in that stuffy room for the greater part of the day from early morning, while Nannie (who is almost stone deaf) read out the newspaper to him. His other sister, Eliza, used to mind the shop. These two old women used to look after him, feed him, and clothe him. The clothing was not difficult, for his ancient, priestly clothes were quite green with age, and his dogskin slippers were everlasting. When he was tired of hearing the news he used to rattle his snuff-box on the arm of his chair to avoid shouting at her, and then he used to make believe to read his Prayer Book. Make believe, because, when Eliza brought him a cup of soup from the kitchen, she had always to waken him.

As I stood looking up at the crape and the card that bore his name I could not realise that he was dead. He seemed like one who could go on living for ever if he only wanted to; his life was so methodical and uneventful. I think he said more to me than to anyone else. He had an egoistic contempt for all women-folk, and suffered all their services to him in polite silence. Of course, neither of his sisters were [*sic*] very intelligent. Nannie, for instance, had been reading out the newspaper to him every day for years, and could read tolerably well, and yet she always spoke of it as the *Freeman's General*. Perhaps he found me more intelligent and honoured me with words for that reason. Nothing, practically nothing, ever occurred to remind him of his former life (I mean friends or visitors), and still he could remember every detail of it in his own fashion. He had studied at the college in Rome, and he taught me to speak Latin in the Italian way. He often put me through the responses of the Mass, he smiling often and pushing huge pinches of snuff up each nostril alternately. When he smiled he used to uncover his big, discoloured teeth, and let his tongue lie on his lower lip. At first this habit of his used to make me feel uneasy. Then I grew used to it.

That evening my aunt visited the house of mourning and took me with her. It was an oppressive summer evening of faded gold. Nannie received us in the hall, and, as it was no use saying anything to her, my aunt shook hands with her for all. We followed the old woman upstairs and into the dead-room. The room, through the lace end of the blind, was suffused with dusky golden light, amid which the candles looked like pale, thin flames. He had been coffined. Nannie gave the lead, and we three knelt down at the foot of the bed. There was no sound in the room for some minutes except the sound of Nannie's mutterings – for she prays noisily. The fancy came to me that the old priest was smiling as he lay there in his coffin.

But, no. When we rose and went up to the head of the bed I saw that he was not smiling. There he lay solemn and copious in his brown habit, his large hands loosely retaining his rosary. His face was very grey and massive, with distended nostrils and circled with scanty white fur. There was a heavy odour in the room – the flowers.

We sat downstairs in the little room behind the shop, my aunt and I and the two sisters. Nannie sat in a corner and said nothing, but her lips moved from speaker to speaker with a painfully intelligent motion. I said nothing either, being too young, but my aunt spoke a good deal, for she is a bit of a gossip – harmless.

"Ah, well! he's gone!"

"To enjoy his eternal reward, Miss Flynn, I'm sure. He was a good and holy man."

"He was a good man, but, you see . . . he was a disappointed man. . . . You see, his life was, you might say, crossed."

"Ah, yes! I know what you mean," [*sic*]

"Not that he was anyway mad, as you know yourself, but he was always a little queer. Even when we were all growing up together he was queer. One time he didn't speak hardly for a month. You know, he was that kind always."

"Perhaps he read too much, Miss Flynn?"

"O, he read a good deal, but not latterly. But it was his scrupulousness, I think, affected his mind. The duties of the priesthood were too much for him."

"Did he . . . peacefully?"

"O, quite peacefully, ma'am. You couldn't tell when the breath went out of him. He had a beautiful death, God be praised."

"And everything . . .?"

"Father O'Rourke was in with him yesterday and gave him the Last Sacrament."

"He knew then?"

"Yes; he was quite resigned."

Nannie gave a sleepy nod and looked ashamed.

"Poor Nannie," said her sister, "she's worn out. All the work we had, getting in a woman, and laying him out; and then the coffin and arranging about the funeral. God knows we did all we could, as poor as we are. We wouldn't see him want anything at the last."

"Indeed you were both very kind to him while he lived."

"Ah, poor James; he was no great trouble to us. You wouldn't hear him in the house no more than now. Still I know he's gone and all that. . . . I won't be bringing him in his soup any more, nor Nannie reading him the paper, nor you, ma'am, bringing him his snuff. How he liked that snuff! Poor James!"

"O, yes, you'll miss him in a day or two more than you do now."

Silence invaded the room until memory reawakened it, Eliza speaking slowly –

"It was that chalice he broke. . . . Of course, it was all right. I mean it contained nothing. But still . . . They say it was the boy's fault. But poor James was so nervous, God be merciful to him."

"Yes, Miss Flynn, I heard that . . . about the chalice. . . He . . . his mind was a bit affected by that."

"He began to mope by himself, talking to no one, and wandering about. Often he couldn't be found. One night he was wanted, and they looked high up and low down and couldn't find him. Then the clerk suggested the chapel. So they opened the chapel (it was late at night), and brought in a light to look for him. . . And there, sure enough, he was, sitting in his confession-box in the dark, wide awake, and laughing like softly to himself. Then they knew something was wrong."

"God rest his soul!"

CHAPTER ONE

1. James Joyce, "Ibsen's New Drama," *Fortnightly Review*, N.S. LXVII. 400 (April 1, 1900), 575–590.

2. John J. Slocum and Herbert Cahoon, *A Bibliography of James Joyce (1882–1941)* (New Haven: Yale University Press, 1953), pp. 150–153, section E-IIa vii–ix. Future footnote references to this book will cite Slocum-Cahoon and give section designations only.

3. James Joyce, "The Day of the Rabblement," in *Two Essays* (Dublin: Gerrard Bros., n.d.).

4. Letter in the Yale University Library. Herbert Gorman, *James*

Joyce (New York: Rinehart & Company, Inc., 1948), p. 68, gives the name of the lost play as *A Brilliant Career*.

5. *Ibid.*, letter from Archer.

6. Arthur Power, *From the Old Waterford House* (London: Mellifont Press Limited, n.d.), pp. 62–67.

7. *Stephen Hero*, ed. Theodore Spencer (New York: New Directions, 1944), pp. 226–230.

8. *Ibid.*, pp. 37, 194, 214.

9. Gorman, *James Joyce*, p. 74.

10. *Ulysses*, pp. 189–90. I take the references to Stephen here to be at least partly autobiographical.

11. Stanislaus Joyce, "Introduction," to *The Early Joyce: The Book Reviews, 1902–1903*, ed. Stanislaus Joyce and Ellsworth Mason (Colorado Springs: The Mamalujo Press, 1955), p. 1.

12. Letter (undated), in the Yale University Library.

13. Letter, dated December 18, 1902, in the Yale University Library.

14. Letter dated October 2 [1904], in the Yale University Library. The year "1904" has been added in pencil.

15. Bernard Gheerbrant, ed., *James Joyce: Sa Vie, Son Œuvre, Son Rayonnement* (Paris: Librairie La Hune, 1949), p. 55.

16. "The Sisters" appeared on August 13, 1904, and "After the Race" and "Eveline" followed before the year was out.

17. Gorman, *James Joyce*, pp. 116–117.

18. Unpublished letter dated October 2 [1904], in the Yale University Library.

19. F. S. Skeffington, postcard dated 29–9–3, in the Yale University Library.

20. Silvio Benco, "James Joyce in Trieste," *The Bookman*, LXXII (December, 1930), 375–380; Stanislaus Joyce, *Recollections of James Joyce by His Brother* (New York: The James Joyce Society, 1950), pp. 24–31.

21. Most of the factual material of this paragraph I have taken from Gorman, *James Joyce*.

22. The Pinker file in the Berg Collection of the New York Public Library contains an interesting collection of letters from publishers rejecting Joyce's early works.

23. Unsigned and undated report written on stationery of Duckworth & Co. Ltd. It was sent to James B. Pinker, Joyce's agent, by Herbert J. Cape with a covering letter dated January 26, 1916. Lord Horder, the present Director of Gerald Duckworth & Co., suggests that the reader may have been Edward Garnett. The report, now in the Yale University Library, is published with the kind permission of Lord Horder and of the Library.

24. Ezra Pound, unpublished letter to James B. Pinker, dated January 30, 1916, now in the Yale University Library. Ezra and Dorothy Pound and the Yale University Library have generously consented to its publication here.

25. *My Brother's Keeper*, p. 199.

26. Arthur Walton Litz, "The Evolution of James Joyce's Style and Technique from 1918 to 1932," a doctoral dissertation completed at Merton College, Oxford, and available on microfilm in typescript from the Wayne University Library; see also, Walton Litz, "Early Vestiges of Joyce's *Ulysses*," *PMLA*, LXXI (March, 1956), 51–60.

27. James Joyce, *Epiphanies*, ed. O. A. Silverman (Buffalo: University of Buffalo, 1956), pp. 6 and 20.

28. Hugh Kenner, "The Portrait in Perspective," in *James Joyce: Two Decades of Criticism*, ed. Seon Givens (New York: Vanguard Press, 1948). This material has been incorporated in Mr. Kenner's book, *Dublin's Joyce* (Bloomington: Indiana University Press, 1956), Chapter 8.

CHAPTER TWO

1. John Livingston Lowes, *The Road to Xanadu: A Study in the Ways of the Imagination* (Boston: Houghton Mifflin Company, 1927), pp. 36–37.

2. Stanislaus Joyce, *Recollections of James Joyce by His Brother* (New York: The James Joyce Society, 1950); Padraic Colum, "Portrait of James Joyce," *The Dublin Magazine*, VII (April–June, 1932), 40–48; Thomas E. Connolly, *The Personal Library*

of James Joyce: A Descriptive Bibliography (Buffalo: University of Buffalo Monographs in English, No. 6 (April), 1955).

3. Herbert Gorman, *James Joyce* (New York: Rinehart & Company, 1948), p. 145 *et passim.*

4. James Joyce, *Finnegans Wake* (New York: The Viking Press, 1939), pp. 169–195.

5. James Joyce, *A Portrait of the Artist as a Young Man* (New York: The Modern Library, 1928), Chapter II.

6. James Joyce, *Ulysses* (New York: The Modern Library, 1934), p. 49.

7. Gorman, *James Joyce*, p. 73.

8. James Joyce, *Stephen Hero*, ed. Theodore Spencer (New York: New Directions, 1944), p. 158.

9. This Ms. draft, formerly in the collection of Mr. John J. Slocum, is now at Yale University.

10. In August, 1906, Joyce was still revising "A Painful Case." "The Dead," the last story written for the collection, was conceived in Rome and probably not finished until late in 1907. See Gorman, pp. 169 and 176.

11. Gorman, pp. 125–127.

12. Silvio Benco, "James Joyce in Trieste," *Bookman*, LXXII (December, 1930), 376; Padraic Colum, "Portrait of James Joyce," *Dublin Magazine*, VII (April–June, 1932), 40–43.

13. On the other hand, Joyce's handling of the theme of marriage in "The Dead" and in two of his later poems, "She Weeps over Rahoon" and "Tutto è Sciolto," as Professor W. Y. Tindall has suggested to me, may indicate hidden trouble in his relationship with Nora: see also Maurice Beebe, "James Joyce: Barnacle Goose and Lapwing," *PMLA*, LXXI (June, 1956), 302–320.

14. Friedrich Nietzsche, *Also Sprach Zarathustra* (New York: Frederick Ungar Publishing Co., n.d.), pp. 60–61.

15. *Ibid.*, p. 68.

16. *Ibid.*, p. 103.

17. *Ibid.*, p. 317.

18. *Ibid.*, p. 104.

19. *Ibid.*, p. 70.

20. Gorman, pp. 73–74.

21. Gerhart Hauptmann, *Michael Kramer*, in *Das Gesammelte Werk* (Berlin: Suhrkamp Verlag, 1943), III, 379.

22. *Ibid.*, pp. 387–388.

23. *Ibid.*, p. 389.

24. *Ibid.*, pp. 394–395.

25. *Ibid.*, p. 392.

26. *Ibid.*, pp. 436–439.

27. *Ibid.*, pp. 440–441.

28. *Ibid.*, p. 433.

29. Stanislaus Joyce, "The Background to 'Dubliners,' " *The Listener*, LI (March 25, 1954), 526.

30. Slocum-Cahoon, E-11a, viii and ix.

31. I have used the translation of this play by Leonard Bloomfield in *Poet Lore*, XX (July–August, 1909), 241–315.

32. James Joyce, "The Day of the Rabblement," in *Two Essays* (Dublin: Gerrard Bros., n.d.). The author dates the essay October 15, 1901.

33. Slocum-Cahoon, E-2e, i.

34. *Before Sunrise*, p. 247.

35. *Ibid.*

36. *Ibid.*, pp. 258–261.

37. *Ibid.*, p. 284.

38. See Richard Ellmann, "The Limits of Joyce's Naturalism," *The Sewanee Review*, LXIII (1955), 567–575.

39. Leo Taxil, *Calotte et Calotins: Histoire Illustrée du Clergé et des Congrégations*, 3 vols. (Paris, ca. 1880).

40. Taxil, *Calotte*, II, 8.

41. *Ibid.*, p. 51.

42. *Ibid.*, p. 52.

43. Leo Taxil, *La Vie de Jésus* (Paris, 1884).

44. For the working out of the Don Giovanni theme, see Vernon Hall Jr., "Joyce's Use of Da Ponte and Mozart's 'Don Giovanni,' " *PMLA*, LXVI (March, 1951), 78–84.

45. The cartoon of the resurrection from Taxil's anticlerical collection may well have been the origin of Stephen's blasphemous remarks. See also the scurrilous stanza in *Ulysses*, pp. 20–21.

46. *Stephen Hero*, pp. 133, 189. It is interesting, though perhaps not significant from Joyce's point of view, to note that Taxil issued in 1889 *La Ménagerie Républicaine*, a series of cartoons in color, each one devoted to a caricature of a leading figure in French affairs, in which the person is represented as the animal he most closely resembles physically or morally. Published after Taxil's reconversion to Catholicism, the book is especially hard on Renan, whom Taxil accuses of blasphemy, pornography, and license. Taxil represents Renan as a smelly goat – half-man, half-animal – an anticipation of the motif of change in the Proteus episode to be discussed below. The supreme hypocrite, Taxil, heaps abuse upon Renan for all the sins of which he himself is guilty.

47. Virag's remarks (U 508), "I am Virag who disclosed the sex secrets of monks and maidens. Why I left the Church of Rome. Read the Priest, the Woman and the Confessional," could without much alteration be made to conform to the titles of several of Taxil's anticlerical diatribes.

48. E. P. Evans, "A Survival of Mediaeval Credulity," *Popular Science Monthly*, LVI (March and April, 1900), 577–586, 706–715; Henry Charles Lea, "An Anti-Masonic Mystification," *Lippincott's Magazine*, LXVI (December, 1900), 948–960. My information concerning details of Taxil's career, unless otherwise attributed, is drawn from these articles.

49. Leo Taxil, *Confessions d'un Ex-Libre-Penseur* (Paris, n.d.); Taxil gives the date of completion as 25 December, 1886.

50. *Ibid.*

51. This early version is in the collection of Joyce's "epiphanies" at the Lockwood Memorial Library of the University of Buffalo. See O. A. Silverman, ed., *Epiphanies*.

52. Taxil, *Confessions*, pp. 364–365.

53. Lea, p. 960.

54. *The Catholic Encyclopedia*, 1913 edition, VII, 701.

55. Homer, *The Odyssey*, trans. by E. V. Rieu (New York, 1946), p. 63.

56. *The Odyssey*, p. 64.

57. Jean Drault, *Drumont: La France Juive et La Libre Parole* (Paris 1935).

58. *Ibid.*, p. 120.

59. *Ibid.*

60. Leo Taxil, *Monsieur Drumont: Étude psychologique* (Paris, n.d.), introduction.

61. *Ibid.*, pp. 1, 2.

62. *Ibid.*

63. Leonard Albert, "Ulysses, Cannibals and Freemasons," *A.D.*, II (Autumn, 1951), 265–283.

64. *Ibid.*, p. 283.

CHAPTER THREE

1. Arthur Power, *From the Old Waterford House* (London: Mellifont Press Limited, n.d.), pp. 62 ff.

2. James Joyce, letter to Grant Richards, dated June 23, 1906, in the Berg Collection of the New York Public Library. Excerpts from this letter were originally published with the generous consent of the Berg Collection and of the Administrators of the Joyce estate.

3. William Archer, letter to James Joyce, dated 15 September, 1900, in the Yale University Library.

4. The story appeared under the heading of "Our Weekly Story" in the magazine dated August 13, 1904.

5. Hugh Kenner, *Dublin's Joyce* (Bloomington: Indiana University Press, 1956), pp. 50–53.

6. This draft is now in the Joyce Collection of the Yale University Library and is identified in the Slocum-Cahoon *Bibliography* as E2a.

7. James Joyce, *Ibsen's New Drama* (London: Ulysses Bookshop, n.d.), p. 3; this essay first appeared in the *Fortnightly Review* of April, 1900.

8. James Joyce, letter to Grant Richards, dated May 5, 1906. The entire letter is reprinted in Gorman, *James Joyce* (New York: Rinehart & Company, Inc., 1948), pp. 149–151.

9. After writing these words, I found in a newly published and brilliantly conceived study by Brewster Ghiselin many of the answers toward which I had been groping. See Ghiselin's "The Unity of Joyce's 'Dubliners,' " *Accent*, XVI (Spring and Summer, 1956), 75–88, 196–213.

10. Kenner, *Dublin's Joyce*, p. 50.

11. See footnote 9 above.

12. The manuscript versions, listed by Slocum-Cahoon as E2e, i and E2e, ii, are both in the Yale University Library.

13. For an account of Joyce's interest in the names of his books, see Eugene Jolas, "My Friend James Joyce," in *James Joyce: Two Decades of Criticism*, ed. Seon Givens (New York: Vanguard Press, 1948).

14. Stanislaus Joyce, "The Background to 'Dubliners,' " *The Listener*, LI (March 25, 1954), 526.

15. Joyce's elopement and its influence on his writing has been treated by many critics, most recently and ingeniously by Maurice Beebe, "James Joyce: Barnacle Goose and Lapwing," *PMLA*, LXXI (June, 1956), 302–320.

CHAPTER FOUR

1. James Joyce, *Stephen Hero*, ed. Theodore Spencer (New York: New Directions, 1944), "Introduction," pp. 7–19.

2. Joseph Prescott, "James Joyce's 'Stephen Hero,' " *The Journal of English and Germanic Philology*, LIII (April, 1954), 214–223.

3. Philip L. Handler, "James Joyce: From Hero to Artist," unpublished Master's essay, Columbia University, 1955.

4. Stanislaus Joyce, *Recollections of James Joyce by His Brother*, (New York: The James Joyce Society, 1950), p. 20.

5. These drafts may be seen in the James Joyce Collection of the Yale University Library; they are also described in John J. Slocum and Herbert Cahoon, *A Bibliography of James Joyce (1882–1941)* (New Haven: Yale University Press, 1953).

6. Many of these letters are published in Herbert Gorman's *James Joyce* (New York: Rinehart & Company, 1948), beginning on p. 146. Other letters from Joyce to Richards are in the Houghton Library of Harvard College and in the Berg Collection of the New York Public Library.

7. Prescott, *op. cit.*, p. 214; *Stephen Hero*, pp. 7–9.

8. J. F. Byrne, *Silent Years: An Autobiography with Memoirs of James Joyce and Our Ireland* (New York: Farrar, Straus and Young, 1953), pp. 35–37.

9. William York Tindall, *The Literary Symbol* (New York: Columbia University Press, 1955), pp. 78 ff.

10. Ghiselin's study appeared in *Accent: A Quarterly of New Literature*, XVI (Spring and Summer, 1956).

CHAPTER FIVE

1. D. S. Mirsky, "Joyce and Irish Literature," *New Masses*, XI (April 3, 1934), 31.

2. *Ibid.*, p. 33.

3. For Joyce's thinly disguised discussion of his struggle against the middle class, see James Joyce, *Finnegans Wake* (New York: The Viking Press, 1939), Chapter VII, pp. 169–195.

4. Slocum-Cahoon lists no known manuscript copy of the story.

5. James Joyce, "Eveline," *The Irish Homestead*, X (September 10, 1904), 761; the story is signed "Stephen Daedalus."

6. This chapter was written before the publication of Brewster Ghiselin's "The Unity of Joyce's 'Dubliners,' " in *Accent* (Spring and Summer, 1956). The article does include a sensitive treatment of "Grace."

7. Stanislaus Joyce, *Recollections of James Joyce by His Brother* (New York: The James Joyce Society, 1950), p. 20.

8. Miles L. Hanley, *Word Index to James Joyce's 'Ulysses'* (Madison: University of Wisconsin Press, 1937).

9. Cf. James Joyce, *Stephen Hero* (New York: New Directions, 1944), p. 64.

10. James Joyce, letter to Robert McAlmon, dated February 11, 1922, in the possession of Mr. Norman Holmes Pearson at Yale University.